Jerry Fite

Safe-guarding Your Love Affair with the Bottle

A tongue-in-cheek approach to getting sober

CompCare Publishers

2415 Annapolis Lane
Minneapolis, Minnesota 55441

Fite, Jerry.
    Safeguarding your love affair with the bottle : a tongue-in-cheek approach to getting sober / by Jerry Fite.
        p.   cm.
    ISBN 0-89638-148-X : $6.95
    1. Alcoholism—Anecdotes, facetiae, satire, etc.
2. Alcoholics-Rehabilitation—United States.   I. Title.
HV5060.F66   1988   88-2621
362.2'92'0207—dc19   CIP

Cover design by Lillian E. Svec

Inquiries, orders, and catalog requests should be addressed to
CompCare Publishers
2415 Annapolis Lane
Minneapolis, Minnesota 55441
Call toll free 800/328-3330
(Minnesota residents 559-4800)

5   4   3   2   1
92   91   90   89   88

To Emmy, and to our children, David and Melissa,
and to my parents, Helen and Horace

Contents

A Note from the Author

1   You're in Good Company   1

2   Diagnosing Yourself   5

3   Finding the Right Environment   31

4   Fortifying Your Defenses   39

5   Developing Your Personality   53

6   Maintaining the Proper Attitude   69

7   Casting Out Spiritual Beliefs   77

8   Getting Off the Wagon   83

9   My Own Story   95

Appendices:

A.   Are You an Alcoholic?   117
B.   Understanding Alcoholism   121
C.   The Statistics on Alcoholism   131
D.   Personalized Disease Chart   133
E.   Where to Go for Help   137

About the Author   141

A Note from the Author

The purpose of this book is to accompany the reader on a journey through the thought processes and the decision-making apparatus of the alcoholic mind. We will be traveling through territory where most things, much of the time, are backward and upside down.

Our starting point is a vaguely defined place where social drinking has begun its transformation into problem drinking. We have three possible destinations: death, institutionalization, or a return to emotional and physical health. We will make all the logic-defying stops along the way, but we won't know where we're going until we get there.

I realize that some of the humor included in this account may not seem funny to those whose pain is intense from trying to love an alcoholic; nor may those who have suffered a lifetime with an active alcoholic be inclined to provide the support, love and forgiveness necessary for the recovery of everyone the disease affects.

Nevertheless, I believe—and pray—that we'll all be a bit stronger in our sobriety and in our serenity at journey's end.

1

You're in Good Company

It's about time somebody stood up for people who enjoy drinking alcoholic beverages.

Don't get me wrong. I don't like drunks, and I'll bet you don't either. In fact, if you're like me, you have no use for people who can't handle booze. They give all of us drinkers a bad name.

I'm sure you join me in deploring irresponsible drinking, the kind that leads to automobile accidents (especially among teenagers), crime, violence, illness, family and financial problems, and so forth. And, I'm equally certain you would have the good sense to stop drinking if —God forbid—these things started happening to you.

But why should you, who may on occasion become a bit tipsy, be painted with the same broad brush (especially by family members and so-called friends) as honest-to-God alcoholics?

Let's set the record straight. Most people who drink do not become alcoholics. Only about one out of every five or six drinkers, depending on whose statistics you accept, eventually becomes addicted to alcohol and/or other substances. You've got to like those odds. I always did.

The vast majority of people who use alcohol do so appropriately and, in the opinion of a few medical experts, beneficially. I'm sure you've seen the periodic medical studies that prove a nightcap, for example, can help reduce stress and anxiety, thereby lowering blood pressure and improving circulation.

I know about these studies because I used to clip them out and post them on the refrigerator door, right next to the articles about alcoholism my wife had put there. Talk about being irrational about booze. I'll bet my wife spent twice as much for cute little magnets to attach quit-drinking messages to the refrigerator door as I did for the booze I kept inside the refrigerator.

Why is it that everybody seems to focus on the negative aspects of alcohol? Other products are at least as dangerous—maybe more so.

Walk into almost any store that sells food and you're confronted by an awesome array of items teeming with sugar and salt. Millions of people suffer from obesity and severe illnesses because of these products. But where's the movement to ban sweets and salt because some people misuse them?

It doesn't take a graduate degree to appreciate some of the social and cultural contributions the use of alcohol has helped make possible. In fact, I've made quite a list of them.

Many great literary figures were prodigious drinkers and connoisseurs of cocaine, heroin, opium and marijuana. Robert Louis Stevenson, Sir Arthur Conan Doyle, Edgar Allen Poe, F. Scott Fitzgerald—the list is long of literary giants who used alcohol and other drugs. I know that some of them ended up as drunks or addicts, but not all of them. I'd rather remember the ones who didn't.

Actors, actresses, singers, dancers, sculptors, composers, painters—great numbers of these creative artists—rival writers in using alcohol and other chemicals trying to unleash their dazzling talents. Few do a better job of it than actors.

How about many of the Hollywood greats— Humphrey Bogart, Spencer Tracy, Ingrid Bergman, Erroll Flynn, Montgomery Clift, Susan Hayward, et al? Their drinking exploits were almost as legendary as their performances on film. It's just a strange coincidence that they died alcohol-related deaths—isn't it?

The evidence that the use of alcohol has gone hand in hand with stellar performances should be overwhelming. But just in case you require more proof, there is one more area that should clinch the argument. Sports. Babe Ruth was no prude about guzzling a few before and after baseball games, and his record needs no apologies. In fact, it is easy to compile an all-star team of notable drinkers in any sport. You might bring that up the next time your spouse grouses about drinking hurting your job performance.

*   *   *

"I agree with everything you're talking about," you may say at this point, "but my husband/wife/lover/parent/child/relative/friend/employer (choose as many as you wish) just won't listen to those stories you've just presented. They'll talk instead about all the movie stars and writers and sports figures and politicians who have gone into alcohol treatment programs or have died of alcoholism without receiving help. Then they'll go right on making my life miserable by telling me all the things they'll do if I don't stop drinking. I'm not obsessed by booze, but sometimes I think they are."

Wonderful. I hope your friends and family members who object to your drinking habits *do* raise these kinds of issues. You can have some dandy responses ready.

First, you can say that you're happy all this attention *is* being given to alcoholics and alcoholism. Thank goodness so many treatment programs are now available for the unfortunate people who need them.

Your point, of course, is that the people who go into treatment for alcoholism, whether they're movie stars or

Your point, of course, is that the people who go into treatment for alcoholism, whether they're movie stars or sports heroes or the next-door neighbor, are probably real alcoholics—quite unlike yourself. If you ever need that kind of help, you can say, you'll sign yourself up for as long as it takes to help you return to normal drinking.

If that's not good enough, here's the clincher. If someone close to you is constantly trying to convince you to cut down on your drinking, the chances are that a disease involving alcohol is present. However, it may not be you who is sick! A nondrinker who is obsessed by another person's use of alcohol is as sick as, or sicker than, the drinker, even according to alcoholism treatment experts. Feel free to use this bit of good news in any manner you wish. It's the truth, and anyone who knows anything about alcoholism will verify it. Simply put, turn the tables on your accusers. It just may work.

By now, hopefully, you have convinced those concerned about your drinking that you're not an alcoholic, that many famous people drink alcohol, that alcohol temporarily helps to relieve stress and anxiety and promotes creativity, and if they keep bothering you about it, they're sick.

If your loved ones are still not convinced, keep reading. You're about to learn how to continue drinking as much as you like as often as you like for as long as you like. Despite the best arguments of the folks who care about you, you can safeguard your love affair with the bottle and avoid sobriety—no matter what it costs.

2
Diagnosing Yourself

"I'm only worried about your health" is one of the first arguments people who claim to care about us will use in their attempts to induce us to stop drinking.

That's a bunch of hogwash, as we all know. If our friends and families were really concerned about our health, they'd stop nagging us to death and let us enjoy our drinking in peace, right?

Nevertheless, many people who like an occasional cocktail or six tend to neglect their general health. They're afraid to go to the doctor, it seems, because they may receive a lecture on their drinking habits. They may be told to cut down or even stop altogether.

Indeed, the chances of receiving such drastic medical advice are becoming greater each year, as the medical profession focuses more attention on the effects of alcohol on the body. But there is no great cause for alarm—at least not yet. Alcohol abuse, alcoholism, and the entire range of chemical dependencies continue to receive relatively little attention in medical schools. Even antiquated diseases like smallpox receive more attention. Since doctors, by and large, are not trained to recognize and treat alcoholism as a primary disease, the chances are pretty good that your doctor will not view your drinking habits as a great source of concern. Besides, it's a free country. If your doctor should make an issue of your drinking, there's no law against finding another doctor—

one with a view toward alcohol which is more compatible with yours.

Another reassuring medical fact for the person determined to protect his or her right to drink is that negative physical effects of alcohol frequently—and conveniently—hide behind other legitimate ailments. Therefore, you may be diagnosed and receive treatment for high blood pressure, or liver problems, or kidney problems, or gastritis, or any number of other maladies, and continue to feel free to maintain your established drinking pattern, even though your physical problem probably would not be present if you did not drink excessively.

Another layer of protection between the drinker and a medical directive to halt the intake of booze is that some physicians may feel it would be insulting to the patient and to his or her family to mention alcohol as a problem. The old social taboo that says it's okay to drink but disgraceful to be a drunk can be most helpful in some doctor/drinker relationships.

Our own ingenuity can be used against a doctor's diagnostic skills with great effect. When we're not under the influence of too much alcohol (or sometimes, even when we are), we are capable of presenting ourselves in such an intelligent, competent manner that heavy drinking or alcoholism simply does not appear to be a likely problem for us. We don't, in other words, fit the stereotypes most folks have of people with "drinking problems."

Some physicians simply don't like to treat alcoholics or heavy drinkers. They may have had little success in helping their patients stop drinking. And for some, the behavior of intoxicated patients may be difficult to endure.

One thing we should always remember is that doctors are also human beings. We may, with a little effort, locate a physician who shares a commitment to unrestrained drinking. Statistics show, in fact, that the rate of alcoholism among doctors is higher than within the general population. Think about it. It may be worth a shot.

Finally, there are those in the medical profession who simply deny that alcoholism is a disease. They usually contend that the drinker has made a conscious decision to put alcohol into his or her body and refuses to stop doing so in spite of physical damage. This doctor may eventually refer you to a psychologist, where you'll have the opportunity to come up with a whole new set of rationalizations and defenses.

At any rate, while we drinkers may never persuade the American Medical Association to stamp "Approved by the AMA" on the way we use our beverage of choice, there are many nifty things we can do to distort the medical profession's stance on the use of alcohol. And, of course, we may capitalize on the considerable disagreement and confusion among medical doctors about alcohol use and its physical consequences to protect our freedom to drink. With a little creative misdirection and a few study results taken out of context, we can make it seem to our friends and families that even if a doctor didn't *prescribe* drinking for us, a doctor at least didn't *proscribe* it.

Sooner or later, we will be forced to tackle a couple of potentially painful key issues head-on: Is alcoholism a disease? Am I a potential alcoholic? We may as well do it now. Fetch a refill and find a comfortable seat, if you'd like.

Yes, alcoholism is a disease. Make no mistake about it. The AMA doesn't equivocate on this point.

Don't stop reading. I'm with you. And I'm not calling you an alcoholic. Rather, I'm helping you find ways to quiet the claims of people who may be suggesting that you *are* on the road to alcoholism. This bit of seemingly bad news is necessary for us to hear because, to protect our drinking, we must be tuned in to the arguments that may be used against it. This is a common rule of debate. And, everyone knows that drinkers are world-class debaters.

Diseases have causes, symptoms and patterns. Usually, diseases are caused by one or a combination of factors. For example, a disease may be caused by environmental factors (coal miners frequently contract black lung disease). Other diseases, such as many types of influenza, may be caused by infectious factors, and we may inherit certain disease predispositions (such as diabetes and hemophilia) from our parents.

We know we have a disease when we don't feel good and we go to a doctor and tell him or her where and when it hurts. The doctor takes a stethoscope and applies it to your chest, says "Hmmm" a number of times, studies your family history, asks a few questions about where you work and what kinds of sick people you've been hanging out with, and then retires to look up things in a book. A few minutes later, the doctor comes back, tells you what you've got, and what you have to do to get better. The doctor has simply identified the causes, symptoms and patterns of your disease. That's how diseases and doctors work.

*   *   *

The causes of alcoholism are somewhat mysterious, which reinforces our case tremendously. Alcoholism is like cancer in many ways. We know several things which probably help to cause both cancer and alcoholism, but it's difficult to isolate one particular culprit. More than likely, two or three or more little causes have conspired to get the job done.

One possible cause of alcoholism is genetic makeup. You inherited it from your parents or from their parents. This is also a great excuse for your drinking habits. Nobody knows for sure exactly how an inherited predisposition toward alcoholism works. In fact, most scientists are still reluctant to come right out and say there is such a genetic link in alcoholism. Most, however, will admit that there is much empirical evidence to support the genetic theory.

Children who have at least one immediate relative who is alcoholic stand a four-times greater chance of being alcoholic than do children who are born to nonalcoholics. This statistic stands up under controlled experiments involving twins who were born to alcoholics but were adopted immediately and reared by nonalcoholics, and other little twists that only researchers could concoct. The standard explanation of the genetic factor in alcoholism is: "There's undoubtedly something there, but we don't know exactly what it is." The message to children of alcoholics seems clear. Don't fool around with pot and booze and stuff or you'll grow up to be like your mother or father. Or, as you undoubtedly prefer, keep right on drinking and put the blame on Mom or Dad.

If you're already a heavy drinker, don't give up on the genetic excuse even if your parents were teetotalers. Just because your folks don't drink and never have doesn't mean they didn't have a predisposition to pass on to you. The world literally teems with people who are sober simply because they never drank in the first place. Do a little climbing around in your family tree, and you're likely to find a hard-drinking grandfather or, at the very least, an uncle who shared your thirst.

There is a consensus that social learning is a primary cause of alcoholism. Most of us have taken grand advantage of the fact that we live in a society that not only expects us to drink, but has almost required us to imbibe if we're to mingle among our peers. That's changing a bit now—to the consternation of true devotees—as it becomes more acceptable to sip soft drinks or expensive bottled water as we observe our friends slipping numbly into the lunchtime or partytime world of blissful incoherency. Were it not for social pressure, in fact, there would probably be millions fewer alcoholics. No matter how it may be disguised with fruit and mixers, most people don't like their first encounter with alcohol. It is, for many, an acquired taste. You have to work at it, like having sufficient dedication to overcome the initial revulsion to inhaling cigarette smoke.

Peer pressure is an incredibly powerful motivator of behavior, particularly among young people. Parents who have watched their child being rejected by other children know how excruciating the pain of not belonging can be. Is it any wonder that a young person's tastes in music, clothing, language and activities follow the path of greatest peer acceptance? And is it fair (or, at the very least, realistic) to expect such a youngster to risk nonacceptance by his or her peers by turning down a beer or a joint? A parental decree to the youngster that simply saying "no" is the solution to present and future drug problems virtually guarantees disobedience. Such a stance almost certainly requires the young person to decide between two no-win alternatives.

Adults should never be too quick to dismiss peer pressure as a cause of chemical addiction among young people. After all, we continue to obey the dictates of peer pressure throughout our lives. We may become more sophisticated in how we express our subservience to peer approval, but we continue to construct many of our attitudes, actions and beliefs according to how they're received by our friends and associates.

Adult peer pressure has the added advantage of not only being real, it may also be a godsend for the drinker. Who can dispute the good intentions of the victimized boozer who says, "Gosh, I'd rather not drink at all. But if you don't have a martini at lunch and a drink after work at my company, you'll never get ahead. Everybody does it except the wimps at the bottom of the pecking order."

Whatever social cause there is to alcoholism, it has a compatible bedperson in psychological causes. Once Bashful Sam finds he's accepted as one of the guys when he downs a six-pack in the school parking lot and doesn't throw up immediately, and also discovers that he has the courage to ask Sally for a date and she accepts because all the fellows say Bashful Sam is one of the guys, he says to himself, "This stuff may taste bad, but it sure does work."

He's also ready to ignore the warnings of his parents, his school counselor, his minister, and the highway patrolman who comes to health class once a year to show pictures of young people bleeding all over wrecked cars. A can of beer does not, as they've tried to tell him, result in an immediate trip to the town gutter. It is a short trip, however, from learning to be comfortable around Sally to applying that knowledge for the next fifty years whenever a stressful situation appears. You and I know, of course, that stressful situations become more and more common as the years go by. Getting out of bed may sooner or later create sufficient trauma to warrant a nip or two. Later on, waking up will do it. The importance of keeping a jug at bedside eventually becomes apparent to many of us. Stress and nerves, you know.

The beauty of being psychologically dependent on booze is that you never run out of excuses to drink.

You've learned to drink to deal with stressful situations. At some point, stressful situations may be caused by your drinking, and you need to drink more to deal with the stress, which creates more stress. By now, many alcoholics are ready for their first trip to the shrink because they are suffering from (you guessed it) stress.

If you are less than candid about your alcohol consumption, the psychiatrist may immediately concur in your self-diagnosis, largely because your hands are shaking, you're sweating all over, your face is red, and you are extremely anxious or depressed, or both. If you're lucky, he or she will say, "Take these," and you can switch your psychological addiction from booze to miraculous little pills. When you take pills, you may find that you do not shake quite so much (at least for a while) and your breath smells better, but you may suddenly find yourself watching creepy crawling things appear on your walls and you may suspect that the entire population of Sicily is out to get you. But you've probably managed to get your family and friends to stop bugging you about drinking for the time being because everybody will believe you're doing something about your drinking problem.

Incidentally, if the first psychiatrist won't buy your self-diagnosis, just keep switching doctors until you find one who will, just like you did with your physician.

There is also a solid group of experts who support the theory that alcoholism is caused by something in our physiological makeup. This differs from genetic causes in that physiological factors may not necessarily have been present in one's parents.

One of the most interesting of the new physiological theories floating around involves a curious breed of rat and some substances called tetrahydroisoquinolines, or TIQs. It seems that a bunch of rats changed their beverage of choice from water to alcohol when scientists injected TIQs into their brains. Further, alcoholics and intoxicated people show higher levels of TIQs in their cerebrospinal fluids than do nondrinkers. One possible conclusion: TIQs cause alcoholism.

Regardless of the validity of the TIQs connection, the theory makes a couple of intriguing arguments available to the heavy drinker. First, if anyone questions the amount or result of our alcoholic intake, we can say, "I'm sorry, but there's nothing I can do about it. I was born with TIQs in my brain, you know." Or, to others or to ourselves, we can say, "Why stop drinking? Now that they've discovered TIQs, it's only a matter of time until they figure out how to remove them. By the time I'm in danger of becoming an alcoholic, they'll know how to prevent it. Isn't science wonderful?"

Another cause that people who work with alcoholics bandy about is spirituality, or the lack of it. If you're among those of us who agree to go to Alcoholics Anonymous meetings on occasion so the family will be placated, I'm sure you've run into this theory. Alcoholics are capable of spending long evenings wrapped up in philosophical discussions about God and who drank the last beer. To show you how religious I was during my drinking days, I once carried on a two-hour conversation with God in a hotel room in Minneapolis. He appeared on a wall in my room as I was halfway through my second fifth of the evening. I think our discussion was quite informative. I wish I could remember what we said to one another.

You know deep down, of course, that spirituality has nothing whatsoever to do with your need to drink, but it can be a great scapegoat, suitable for creative and sanctimonious use at a moment's notice. AA members talk a lot about a Higher Power, who seems to possess many of God's qualities, but AA members swear a lot, too. Perhaps a good way to handle the spirituality angle is to stop at a bar after an AA meeting, toss down a few in honor of having done something good for your family, and then report to your wife or husband, with appropriate nonjudgmental sorrow, that you simply can't hang out with people who profess great spiritual powers and then use incredibly foul language in telling horror stories about their drinking. A few direct quotes will help cement your case.

No doubt, alcoholism has many causes, though nobody can really pinpoint a specific cause in each specific case. The lesson for drinkers in this is that it probably isn't a good idea to say, "I don't know why I drink so much." Not when you can blame your genetic makeup, your social situation, how your mind works, your physiology, and your spiritual beliefs.

*   *   *

The next item that a disease requires is a set of symptoms. It's essential that the alcoholic who wishes to continue drinking learn these symptoms thoroughly. Otherwise, your wife or husband may spot you exhibiting one of them, pull out a piece of ever-present anti-drinking literature, and say, "See? You're doing it, just like it says here." Some unfortunate souls are forced to go on the wagon for as long as a month to prove they don't have the symptoms they've just demonstrated.

The most common symptom of alcoholism is the craving for a drink. If you're careful, no one needs to know the craving exists. You may have to settle for lunch at McDonald's on occasion if people start to wonder why you always insist on eating at Joe's Bar and Grill. At home you should get up in the middle of the night at least a few times and not take a nip so your bed partner won't be completely certain a symptom has been spotted. A sure-fire trick, if you can handle it, is to force yourself not to have a few drinks before dinner once or twice a month. You may say, "A drink just doesn't sound good tonight," or something to that effect, and you've just bought yourself several more months of comparatively peaceful liquid relief.

Misdirection and misinformation are invaluable tools for the serious drinker. Not all alcoholics crave their booze in exactly the same way or at the same times. If you don't crave a morning drink, for example, dig into your spouse's Al-Anon literature and find the list of twenty questions which includes morning drinking as a symptom of alcoholism. "Guess that proves it," you can say. "Alcoholics drink in the mornings. I never do that." The same trick works well with binge drinkers or weekend drinkers, who may rarely feel the craving coming on between bouts of uncontrolled intake. "I can take it or leave it," is a useful message to drive home on the nondrinking days.

Another symptom which is a dead giveaway that your drinking has entered the problem zone is blackouts. Don't panic. If you're careful, you're the only one who'll understand exactly what's going on. Most people— probably including those close to you—think that a blackout is the same as passing out. You can use this misunderstanding to your advantage. As a matter of fact, you can twist it so that it's still to your advantage even after other people begin to catch on to the truth.

You experience a blackout when you can't recall exactly what you did while you were drinking. You don't actually pass out; you keep functioning, but have little or no recall of what went on during a certain period of time. Stories of heroic blackouts are legend among AA members. You may have a few of your own.

The most impressive blackouts are those in which the drinker begins his evening in one city and returns to awareness a day or several days later in a strange city. Typically, he or she has no recollection of making the trip, of checking into the hotel, or—frequently—of withdrawing the family's life savings from the bank and spending it. The aroma of an unfamiliar perfume or aftershave lotion from the other half of the bed is, for some, the first indication that a blackout has taken place.

Less exotic blackouts occur all the time. The alcoholic husband, for example, may honestly have no idea why his wife's bags are packed when he awakens the next morning. The last thing he remembers is a rather pleasant and intimate conversation preceding a romantic overture. Why his wife has a black eye and two windows are shattered are a complete mystery to him.

Or the alcoholic wife may awaken with a slightly upset stomach and a minor headache, which are overridden by the pride she feels when she remembers how brilliant her conversation was at last night's party. She can't imagine why her husband has already gone to work without leaving a note, or why his side of the bed is unwrinkled. It dawns on her that something unusual must have taken place when the swinging bachelor down the street —who was also at the party—drops by to return her bra.

In my case, I began to suffer embarrassment the summer I was chosen to coordinate my son's Little League baseball team. One of my primary duties was to schedule games and to arrange makeup dates for games that were rained out. For some strange reason, I began making the same arrangements two and three different times, with the same people, in the space of a few hours. It couldn't have been the fifth of Scotch I needed to face the awesome responsibilities of the job, I decided. I was tired, I hadn't been feeling well, and one's memory does slip as one grows older. I was thirty-eight at the time. My solution was to keep a notepad and pen by the phone, and I was able to keep most teams where they belonged for the rest of the summer.

The arrival of blackouts doesn't necessarily mean you must curtail your drinking. You can explain your behavior to your loved ones, at least the first few times, by pleading exhaustion, job responsibilities, illness, or the effects of medication. "Boy, that tranquilizer really hit me," you can say. "I'll be glad when the pressure at work eases up."

Perhaps the most certain indication that people have become bona fide alcoholics is when they start to lose total control of what happens when they begin drinking. Most of them have admirable control in the early days. So, for folks like you and me, even if we realize that we're drinking more than other people, or that we're drinking in different patterns, we're adept at controlling our behavior so nobody catches on. Sooner or later, unfortunately, we may lose this ability.

A typical scenario of this symptom catching up with us is our conduct at a business party. The boss is having a party for the company's top dozen executives and the half-dozen or so promising young lions who may join the elite group in the near future. You're one of the aspirants. (Alcoholics, for no apparent scientific reason, are frequently highly intelligent, hard-working, creative and personable. We usually start out making good social impressions as well, until the substance that contributes to our social success turns on us.) You and your wife buy new outfits for the occasion, you have a few short ones before leaving so you'll be comfortable and relaxed when you get there, and you talk of the occupational and financial success that is nearly yours as you drive to the party. You have resolved to drink only lightly, showing that while you're one of the crowd, you have no need to drink in order to enjoy yourself. After all, despite the everpresent status of booze at these affairs, you know the company bigwigs toss up the warning flag if a potential vice president shows an inordinate fondness for drink. Everything goes according to plan for an hour or so, but you experience (perhaps for the first time) an inability to stick to your resolve. You drink more, and then your wife is tugging desperately at your sleeve as you demand the attention of the group so they may share your insights into the monetary policies of third world nations. You're pleased when an attractive woman seems particularly engrossed in your discussion, and you make a play for her, even though something in the back of your mind tells you she's the boss's wife. When she suggests that you step outside for some fresh air, you go along willingly, convinced that she has something exciting in mind. Somebody leads your wife down from the upstairs bedroom where she has been crying, and the boss's chauffeur drives the two of you home.

While the grandiosity of an alcoholic is likely to be satisfied by an unforgettable episode such as the one above, loss of control usually occurs in more mundane circumstances. We may be congratulating ourselves—over a twelve-pack at 3:00 A.M.—for keeping our cool when a friend or a coworker said something we didn't like during the day. Suddenly, for some uncontrollable reason, right in the middle of our self-congratulatory thoughts, we pick up the phone and read the riot act to the sleepy offending party, who had no idea that he or she had done anything to upset us.

Loss of control happens when we can no longer predict how much we will drink once we start, or what we will do while we're drinking. People who are not alcoholic may experience this sensation once or twice in a lifetime, but it is so frightening and the consequences are so dire that they won't drink that way again. Alcoholics, of course, don't have that option. And, once loss of control begins, it will become more frequent.

At this point, we may begin to realize just how important alcohol is to us. So, we have to find ways to try even harder to safeguard our love affair with the bottle.

Since we can't stop drinking or change the way we drink, the logical step for us is to stay away from people (and from telephones) when we drink. When we violate this principle, we find ourselves becoming embroiled in violent arguments, barroom brawls, and creating an indelible impression on friends and neighbors. We may also find ourselves intimately knowledgeable of the inner workings of traffic court.

An important thing to remember about the loss of control symptom is that it is not necessarily a dramatic event, as described above. Sometimes the alcoholic is the only one who knows he or she has lost control. Because it can't be seen by others, though, doesn't mean it hasn't happened.

Another symptom that creeps up on us is a change in the amount of alcohol our bodies will tolerate. In the beginning, we may receive a lot of strokes from people for our ability to "handle our liquor."

"Boy, old Red can really put it away," an impressed friend will say. "He's had six and I've had two, and he's sober as a judge. My head's already spinning."

Actually, there's no great secret to this kind of success. We've conditioned ourselves to process ever-increasing volumes of alcohol. Another thing our friends don't realize is that we don't drink such amazing amounts simply because we want to or because we like to show off. We drink in such volume because we have to. Our body chemistry has adjusted to the alcohol we've been feeding it, and like a spoiled child it throws a tantrum when we try to withhold the required daily allowance.

Again, however, we don't have to admit to other people that we're addicted. We can revel in their praise until they catch on that our behavior isn't all that admirable, we can continue to sneak a few drinks when others aren't watching, and we can isolate ourselves.

Ultimately, our incredible tolerance for alcohol will do an abrupt about-face, and we may find ourselves physically unable to consume as much as has been our custom. Don't worry, this doesn't mean that booze is losing its impact on you. It simply means that after years of adjusting heroically, a few vital organs such as the liver and the kidneys have thrown in the towel. They're exhausted from processing all that alcohol and refuse to cooperate anymore. You still become just as drunk as usual, but you don't need to drink as much to reach that point, since more is staying in your body.

While this is bad news from the point of view of your overall physical health, it's good news for your ability to continue to drink in relative peace. You don't have to sneak drinks anymore. In fact, you can very proudly demonstrate to your loved ones that you've cut down your intake by half or more. The typical family will rejoice at the irrefutable evidence that you have suddenly amassed formidable will power and are on the road to returning to sensible drinking. You don't have to tell them about a decrease in tolerance being a primary symptom of severe, chronic alcoholism—that is, if they're still around to listen.

The downfall of many heavy drinkers has come in the form of withdrawal symptoms that are visible for the whole world to see. We can hide these pretty well in the beginning, and there are precautions we can take later on that will minimize them. A simple hangover is a withdrawal symptom that most people who drink experience on occasion. The hangover happens because we've treated our system to more alcohol than it's accustomed to, and it has literally gone haywire while trying to figure out what to do with it all. At that point, our system requires one of two solutions: either let it dry out, or put some more alcohol in. The "hair of the dog"—or drinking to stop a hangover—works because we are satisfying a craving of the body. Most alcoholics will not experience hangovers at all, or will not have severe hangovers, because we maintain a satisfactory level of alcohol for the machinery to hum along contentedly.

The next common withdrawal symptom begins internally and may be concealed from others for a long time, if we make certain we do what is required to control it. We call this symptom the shakes. In the earlier stages, the shakes are usually felt as a sort of free-floating anxiety, bringing with them a huge load of tension. Other people may not see it, but we're literally shaking to pieces on the inside. The body again is telling us that we've neglected to feed it the expected dosage at the right time. The processing organs have caught up with their work of eliminating the alcohol, and they're begging for more. Industrious little rascals, those organs.

Sooner or later, the shakes begin to be quite obvious and more difficult to conceal. We learn very quickly not to offer to bring a fellow worker a cup of coffee if we haven't had our morning fix—the poor guy will get about a half-cup, with the rest spilling on him, on us, or on the floor. It can also be embarrassing if we stop after work with the gang and spill half our first drink on the trip to our mouth.

It is much safer, we soon learn, to have a bottle hidden someplace and take a quick hit or two to calm our nerves before we must display a steady hand in public.

Make no mistake about it—the physical effects of withdrawal can be fatal. Despite all the stories one hears about drying out in jail or in some other institution, doing without booze can be life-threatening in some cases. The DT's (delerium tremens) are down the road a ways from the generic-type shakes, but they do happen, and they can be deadly.

If you are foolish enough to get yourself into this condition, forget about shrugging and going about your business. Somebody's going to notice you (unless you've taken the precaution of hiding yourself away) and you'll probably be taken to a hospital or a clinic someplace. But don't panic—even then this does not have to spell the end of your drinking. With any luck, your friends will take you somewhere for help that will either misdiagnose your problem, decide you need a maintenance diet of tranquilizers, or dry you out and send you on your way.

Now let me reassure you that the compulsion to drink is a symptom that you can keep to yourself with considerable success. Compulsion may or may not be found in the company of a previous symptom, the craving of alcohol. When we crave a drink, we desperately want and/or need it. Compulsion results in our drinking even when we would be comfortable without it. People who drink normally do so because they decide a drink would taste good, because they're among a group of friends who are having a drink, or because they simply feel like relaxing over a cocktail. They cannot relate to the fact that alcoholics *must* drink. We feel compelled to do so, and when the compulsion hits, it must be fulfilled. Some people can relate food, work or sweets to this compulsion, but those things are bush league compared to what we experience. As long as you can hide the frequency and amount of your consumption, other people generally won't detect your compulsion. Since they don't relate to such an experience, they won't suspect you of having it.

The compulsion may strike in different ways, making it even harder to detect. Some binge, or periodic, drinkers, for example, feel compelled to drink only every few days, weeks, or even months. When they do drink, however, it's gangbusters.

Some alcoholics are strictly weekend drinkers. They work hard all week, are considered good, dependable employees, and the boss would (and frequently does) argue hard and long with the spouse who claims the guy is alcoholic. The weekend drinker hides his addiction well, except from his own family. Weekends are typically spent lying on the sofa, alternately drinking, watching sports on TV, and passing out. I was always envious of weekend and binge drinkers. My compulsion was there for anyone to see, since I fed my need several times every day. But how could a guy who spends a lot of time sober be suspected of alcoholism?

The best way to hide your compulsion, again, is to find a way to drink secretly. Nosy family members frequently screw up our best plans, because it's hard to do anything secretly at home. Another alternative is to con a medical doctor or a psychiatrist into prescribing tranquilizers. Pills don't smell on your breath, and they'll tide you over until you can get to the libation of your choice.

There are a number of other symptoms that come packaged in the form of various harmful personal consequences. Symptomatic of alcoholism are, among others: frequent physical and/or mental problems, marital problems and general health problems within the family (even nondrinking family members get "sick" from the disease), social withdrawal by both you and your family, job problems (usually absenteeism and tardiness), financial problems, legal problems, and the deterioration of moral and spiritual values.

The scary part of this is—it doesn't take a genius to figure out what our problem is! All it takes is a little knowledge. Why more people don't peg us sooner is a tribute to their own ignorance, mutual denial of the problem, and to our peculiar brand of cleverness. One thing that helps us continue drinking is that—while we all have many things in common—the drinking pattern and progression may vary from individual to individual, allowing us to throw most people off the track if they seem ready to home in on us.

Some fortunate people, for example, may show few physical symptoms of alcoholism. Their dependency is primarily psychological. Their compulsion to drink is as great as that of people whose entire bodies are shaking, but their tremors are in their minds.

*   *   *

The most common alcoholic pattern involves maintenance drinking on a daily basis. These folks can usually control how much they drink, but they cannot tolerate—physically or psychologically—skipping a day. A steady "glow" is maintained throughout the day, but the person usually is able to function—sometimes quite capably.

Some people are able to maintain this steady but undramatic state of intoxication for a matter of years, with nobody the wiser. In fact, people will become so accustomed to seeing the person in this "normal" state that it never occurs to them that he or she is actually quite drunk—all the time. But the disease progresses, unfortunately, so most maintenance drinkers eventually begin to give off warning signals. The glow, for example, seems to emanate from the nose, and whatever effectiveness breath mints had has been overwhelmed by the sheer force of 100-proof mouthwash.

The periodic drinker, as we mentioned earlier, may go off on awe-inspiring binges that last days or weeks, but this lucky soul also has the ability to remain totally dry for days, weeks, and months at a time. If he could keep his cool, this type of alcoholic could probably slide by for life without being detected. Frequently, however, the two binges per year that he or she has result in bankruptcy, jail, divorce, serious injury, or all of the above, and more. The periodic drinker is no less an alcoholic than the daily drinker. He or she is simply able to fool more of the people more of the time.

If you are a periodic drinker your prognosis for continuing to drink is quite good.

The progression of the loss-of-control drinker typically goes from psychological dependency to physiological dependency. Early on, this person may be able to turn down drinks at will, but loses complete control once he or she takes the first drink. Eventually, he or she usually also loses the ability to refuse the first drink. Nevertheless, this kind of drinker can run out the string for a long time before somebody begins to suspect him or her. You don't need to be disheartened if your pattern is one of the more obvious ones. There are lots of tricks for all of us.

Perhaps the most serious—or hopeless—drinking pattern of all can be seen in the people who get into serious trouble every single time they drink. They imbibe, and within a matter of hours they're in jail, in the hospital with gastritis, involved in an accident, or some other such tragedy. Professionals call these people the "immediate consequence drinkers." No matter what crisis occurs, or its severity, they will return to drinking and another traumatic event will occur as soon as health and the law allow. Even this type of drinker can persevere, though, *if* they can learn to drink in isolation.

*   *   *

Now, let's acquaint ourselves with some facts. It's important to understand the magnitude of what we're up against. First, alcoholism is a primary disease. Alcoholism doesn't happen because something else happened. It's a primary disease in its own right, complete with its own symptoms and path of progression. Other diseases develop secondarily to the primary disease of alcoholism. Doctors aid us considerably in obfuscating the primary nature of alcoholism by writing down liver disease, kidney failure, stroke, heart attack, suicide, death by accident, and myriad other things on our death certificates, when none of these things would have happened without the presence of alcoholism.

Secondly, alcoholism is what people in the alcohol treatment field call a "multi-faceted" disease. In other words, alcoholism doesn't affect us in only one or two ways; it grabs hold of everything. This truly marvelous fact works in our favor, because it's inordinately difficult to treat a person physically, emotionally, psychologically and spiritually. Alcoholism is like a cancer; if you don't get it all, it will thrive again. Because of this, we're able to continue drinking after a doctor has tried to cure our physical complaints and has dried us out, or a shrink has tried to stuff us into the normal range of the Minnesota Multiphasic Personality Inventory, or our spouses and/or lovers have pledged their undying love and devotion if we'll quit drinking, or our ministers have alternately promised streets of gold and fires of hell as our just rewards.

If these folks don't all get together at the same time and cooperate in their approach to us, none of the cures will work. Obviously, people with such varied interests and competencies don't often cooperate, so we're safe unless we're forced into a place that concentrates on all facets of the disease. Even then, as we shall see, the battle is far from lost.

Then, of course, there's the fact that alcoholism is a progressive disease. It doesn't get better by itself. The symptoms and effects of the disease are also predictable, so you can keep tabs on how things are going. I've included in the back of the book one of those dreary charts of progression that alcohol treatment people like to show our families so they'll be scared out of their wits, nod their heads and say, "Yep. That's him all right." They then proceed to make our lives miserable by hanging that stupid chart on the refrigerator door and the bathroom wall. I've included the chart so you can study it and come back with, "Look at this one. I've never done this one."

Alcoholism also fits the definition of a chronic disease, in that it is perpetual (it doesn't ever stop, even when we're not drinking), and it's incurable (it can be put into remission of sorts, but you never get rid of it). It is also an acute disease; every symptom shows up periodically as long as we drink.

Alcoholism is, of course, a potentially fatal disease. If you don't end it all by driving into a tree, you may die from cirrhosis of the liver or some other secondary disease, or you may wind up as a statistic of some mental institution. What nonalcoholics don't understand is that we pretty well know the risks, but *we want to drink* regardless of the consequences. Besides, unless we have an accident, we're not going to die right away. It'll take a few years, probably longer. Maybe we'll quit when the doctor gives us six months to live. On the other hand, that would be a pretty silly time to quit, wouldn't it? Bottoms up.

Finally, alcoholism is the most prevalent disease in the world. You have lots of company. This can be helpful on those occasions when you need to point out someone who is a worse drinker than you are. They're easy to find.

I know a kindly old gentleman in his early seventies who had been forced into a treatment program well before he felt ready to abandon his drinking. He was able to put everybody off for weeks by saying such things as: "Hell, I ain't as bad as a lot of folks. I got a long ways to go yet. I knew a fella back home who used to drink lighter fluid when he couldn't get nothing else. He drank lighter fluid all the time. Hell, I've only drunk lighter fluid once or twice my whole life. When I get that bad, I'll come back and let you fellas give me the cure."

Perhaps the most valuable defense you can muster on short notice includes a few basic denials, a couple of misdiagnoses (by yourself as well as by professionals), and the common misunderstanding most people have about the disease.

The first step, then, is denial. Basic denials include such old standbys as: "I can't be an alcoholic because I only drink beer," ". . . I'm too young; I haven't been drinking all that long," ". . . I've never lost a job," ". . . I've never gotten a DWI," and so on. Use your imagination. I'm sure you can come up with thousands more.

Another tried and true form of denial is blaming other people, places or things for your drinking. "If you weren't such a bitch/bastard, I wouldn't drink," is a sure winner, along with blaming the job, the boss, the neighborhood, the world political situation, and the fact that the St. Louis Cardinals were rained out yesterday.

You don't have to go to a professional for a good misdiagnosis; you can do most of it yourself. Deciding that you're crazy and telling everybody else about it is a dependable standby. You can also decide that you're smarter or more sensitive than other people, or that you simply march to the beat of a different drummer. The drummer, of course, probably drinks lighter fluid.

Professionals can help considerably with misdiagnoses, and they're usually happy to do so. Psychologists and psychiatrists may diagnose alcoholism as a mental disorder, medical doctors may see it as a symptom of anxiety or depression, ministers may see it as a moral issue, and parents, spouses, children and friends— who probably gained their professional knowledge from the professionals listed above—may consider your disease a matter of willpower—or lack of it.

Add a few myths to the existing stack of misunderstandings about alcoholism, and you're ready to face the world with a new determination to drink as much as you like whenever you like.

3

Finding the Right Environment

"It's raining; I need a drink. The sun came out? I'll drink to that."

Sound familiar? It's a shame nobody wants to hire us to invent drinking excuses for them—many of us would be wealthy. Of course, that's part of the unfairness of the world. Youth is wasted on the young, the rich get richer, and people whose drinking is not suspect can drink all they want without making excuses for it.

Actually, I've never understood why we devoted drinkers spend so much time inventing excuses for drinking. I suspect, in fact, that I frequently drew attention to my drinking by attempting to justify or explain it. In effect, I protested too much.

Finding excuses to drink is doubly unnecessary when one considers that there are literally thousands of time-tested excuses already lying around, and surprisingly, most of them are totally accepted by the American public. Imagine a World Series victory celebration without champagne; a wedding without toasts; a company picnic without beer; an intimate dinner without wine. The list goes on. We even have two holidays—St. Patrick's Day and New Year's Eve —devoted almost exclusively to drinking.

Practically every living being in this country grew up or is growing up in a drinking, drug-using society. Seventy percent of the adult population in the United States drink alcoholic beverages, and more than eighty-five million drug prescriptions are filled per year for mood-altering chemicals. The means are readily available, and it is legal and (at least for the time being) socially permissible to maintain a good, strong addiction. We won't even talk about illicit drugs in this chapter. People addicted to illegal drugs, including cocaine, are in a minority. Even street addicts are learning that alcohol and prescription drugs are just as effective as so-called hard drugs, and the law stays off your back when you're legally high, unless you insist on driving while drinking or drugging.

In the meantime, we "respectable" drinkers can stagger along our merry way, knowing that the full force of national and international law is being exerted outward from our borders to cope with the illicit drug traffic, with precious little attention being directed toward alcohol and prescription drug use within our own homeland. One thing we can do to maintain the status quo is to show up periodically at PTA meetings and join in the ongoing ranting and raving about marijuana in students' lockers.

You can be almost correct when you defend your drinking by saying, "Why single me out? Everybody does it." In fact, you would also be more right than wrong if you claimed that it's hard *not* to drink and use drugs in our society. We experience great pressure to participate, beginning at a very early age. And, eventually, we learn to construct a 100-proof environment in which drinking plays a central role. It's an unbeatable combination.

*   *   *

Social pressure to drink and/or take drugs comes from external sources, which usually include our peers, our communities, our cultural surroundings, and the local and national media.

From these various sources, we are told that alcohol and drugs will help us to achieve the "good life," that our vision of romance (read this to mean sex in the case of most advertising) will be fulfilled, and that we can become as popular as our sports and music heroes if we simply indulge in a particular brand of booze.

We can use all these messages to further our habits. I must admit, however, that I developed misgivings about some of them at the height of my athletic glory in college. Having once competed the day after a nighttime bout of drinking, I learned quickly that a particular brand of beer had no positive relationship to quality athletic performance. As a result, I rarely used alcohol until my athletic career was over.

I also had problems associating romantic success with drinking. Maybe other guys knew how to achieve just the right level of intoxication for inhibitions to flee, but either my dates or I kept passing out or throwing up or both. Cleaning up the car the morning after such interludes nipped many of my romances in the bud.

I did learn, however, some things about booze that are true. I was more relaxed in social situations if I had taken a few drinks before they began. Parties became more fun and I felt no noticeable anxiety when meeting new people. I could strike up a conversation more easily, I felt intelligent, I was part of the group, and I found that I could party all night. Fatigue seemed to disappear along with the third or fourth drink.

Most people have undoubtedly discovered that alcohol does have social benefits, but heavy drinkers view revelry as the mother lode of life. We adapt the social benefits of booze to an impressive array of activities: cocktail parties, keggers, dances, picnics, weddings, ball games, hunting and fishing, happy hours, you name it.

For us, the social use of alcohol soon becomes a necessity. We simply don't function socially without it. And, fortunately, we rarely have to function without it, if we choose our events carefully.

*   *   *

Psychological pressures to drink overlap quite conveniently with social pressures. The discovery that we socialize more easily while and after drinking leads to a psychological need to brace oneself a bit before interacting with others.

Even in our early days of heavy drinking, we usually have developed a psychological need for booze. We honestly think we can't face significant parts of life without chemicals. And we have learned that adding alcohol to anxiety or stress, for example, results (at least in the early days) in the reduction of anxiety and stress. This form of behavior reinforcement is quite powerful. Behavior which receives positive rewards is the most quickly learned behavior, and the most difficult to extinguish or modify.

The psychological progression of alcoholism frequently follows the behavioral model quite accurately. Using the example of drinking to ease social awkwardness, we may initially receive positive rewards (less-strained conversation, a feeling of belonging, etc.) each time we drink. Even when drinking starts to cause occasional problems, it still seems to help us frequently enough to fit an intermittent-reward type of reinforcement. Add this kind of ingrained behavior to the addictive qualities of alcohol itself, and it's always party time.

A true appreciation of the "cunning, baffling, and powerful" nature of our drinking may be gained if one contemplates the fact that when booze starts to create more stress and anxiety than it reduces, and begins to cause us to isolate ourselves socially instead of helping us "belong," we develop a psychological need to drink so we can cope with the reality that drinking doesn't work anymore. That's awesome. And somehow comforting to truly committed drinkers.

*　　*　　*

Gradually—if we are smart—we begin to remove all elements of doubt about drinking from our social lives. One sure-fire way to drink in peace is to make your entire environment so filled with drinking activities that your total lifestyle is permeated by alcohol. This isn't hard to do since, as we noted earlier, drugs and alcohol play major roles in our society. Alcoholics will take this already conducive environment and manipulate it even further.

For example, liquor is usually available wherever life's other necessities are sold. "Excuse me, Joe, I have to stop at the market to get some milk . . . might as well pick up a fifth as long as we're here."

If you commute to and from work, it doesn't take much investigation to discover a bar close to a bus stop or a taxi stand. In fact, one consideration bar owners give to the location of their establishments is proximity to commuter waiting areas. It is then an easy thing to have a quick one while waiting for the ride home, and equally easy to start finding excuses to leave work a few minutes early so you "won't miss your bus."

Meeting friends for lunch is always a good time for a few drinks, and you can pass it off as true consideration of friendship if you arrive at the restaurant a little early so you're certain to get a good table. There's no way your friends will know how many drinks you've already had beforehand. This is also a good way for the alcoholic housewife to get away from home for a while and reinforce her image as a social drinker.

These are just a few of the tricks you can take advantage of—and enhance—as you drink as much as you please, when you please. There are dozens more.

The first businessperson ever to don a three-piece suit probably came equipped with the knowledge that better business contacts could be made over martinis at lunch than in a working session at the office. Also, men and women learn that liquor stores and bars near plants and factories are happy to cash payroll checks, and any place that offers dancing, music, billiards or other forms of after-work relaxation also expects a brisk business in alcohol.

We drinkers are masters at cultivating habits based on social, psychological, and environmental conditions (or exotic combinations of the three) to make certain that wherever we are, it would be easier, and often more acceptable, to have a drink than not to have a drink. These may include taking care of loneliness by going to singles bars, treating spouses to dinner out—but only at restaurants that serve liquor—and becoming suave and upwardly-mobile at home by always having a before-dinner cocktail, wine with the meal, and an aperitif afterwards.

Psychologists may argue for centuries about whether we're products of our heredity or our environment, but the outcome doesn't make much difference to us drinkers. We can take anything you give us and turn it into another good excuse to drink.

*   *   *

Unfortunately, as we've perfected our drinking routines, many of our friends, relatives, business associates and others have become knowledgeable about so-called alcoholic behavior, and have learned ways to predict and counteract it. They may say that they understand we have a disease, and that they want to help us gain sobriety. They may even have the ability to make not drinking sound awfully enticing.

Here are a few of the tactics people will use to try to sabotage our carefully cultivated drinking environment.

People who say they care about us will try to get us to develop relationships with "healthy" (to nonalcoholics, "healthy" seems to mean anyone who doesn't drink) individuals and groups.

They'll encourage us to go to church, to AA, and to encounter groups. Our spouses will invite a constant stream of nondrinkers and recovering alcoholics to the house for dinner. We'll suddenly feel as though we're social butterflies, but it won't take long for us to figure out that every time we go to someone else's house for dinner, no drinks are offered before, during or after the meal. And at some point after dinner the host or hostess will casually mention something about alcoholism and we'll sit through a couple of hours of inspirational tapes.

The real danger to our drinking at this point is that we may begin to like these people. Even though they're nondrinkers, most of them won't appear to be fuddyduddies, and some of them will even enjoy dirty stories. Worst of all, their lives will appear to be in order. They'll have nice furniture, and we will begin to suspect that everything is paid for. When you go into one of your tirades that usually sets people to nodding and understanding why a drink is the only possible solution to the issues you raise, these people will sit calmly until you're finished, and return to the subject at hand as if you'd never said a word. They won't appear to be worried about anything.

Chances are if all these pieces seem to fit, you've entered an AA sanctuary.

The only solution is to retreat—quickly.

4
Fortifying Your Defenses

Even those working hardest to reform us will frequently note, with grudging admiration, that we possess many appealing qualities. We drinkers tend to be intelligent, sensitive, generous, and lovable—when we're not drunk. Our well-intentioned family and friends seem to make it a holy mission to return us to sobriety despite ourselves, because they think they see our true selves beneath our drunken exteriors.

They don't understand how we can summon so much will to maintain our drunkenness, when we can't seem to gather enough spunk to string together more than a few days of sobriety at a time. Actually, it seems to them that we must love drinking more than we love them. Little do they know how strong our defenses must be to repel such logic and caring.

A word here for female drinkers as we work to build our defenses. Discussing how to develop effective defenses to protect our drinking is easier for me if I use sports examples and analogies. I hope it will be understood that what may seem to be a male-oriented frame of reference is a result of my limitations, not of chauvinism. For the true aficionado of booze and boozing, there is little room for meaningful sexism anyway—we are all equal before, and under, the bar.

It has become fashionable for professional football teams to give descriptive nicknames to their defensive units, such as the Doomsday Defense of the Dallas

Cowboys, the Orange Crush of the Denver Broncos, the Steel Curtain of the Pittsburgh Steelers, and the Killer B's of the Miami Dolphins. We drinkers also have a nickname for our defense—the Killer D's. Our big-name D's are *Denial, Detour,* and *Delay.*

As I mentioned in the last chapter, the captain of our defense is our biggest, meanest, toughest D—*Denial. Denial* simply refuses to acknowledge any harmful consequences of alcohol abuse, often in the face of seemingly irrefutable evidence to the contrary. The more common forms of Denial include: making the problem the fault of other people, places, things or conditions; defining the problem so the drinker himself or herself is excluded; and minimizing the amount of alcohol used and the consequences of that use.

Here are a few examples, any of which can serve you well in times of stress:

Denial can take one of your problems and hand it off to someone else or something else. With a straight face, Denial can say, "I admit I've been drinking quite a bit lately, but I had two luncheon speeches last week, and I had to let the Johnson boy go, just when his wife was expecting. The stock market isn't doing any good, either. Anybody would drink if they had to deal with pressures like these."

If you watch Denial's moves during a slow motion instant replay you'll notice that he always blames someone else for anything bad he does—no matter how outlandish. Anyone can learn to master these techniques. Get fired? Your boss has it in for you. Fall off the curb and twist your ankle on the way home from happy hour? The city should be sued for not having better streetlights. Get a DWI? The police are out to get you.

Denial is an absolute genius at shifting attention from drinking to job problems. "Why am I getting drunk again, tonight? I'll tell you why I'm getting drunk again tonight. It's because I had the idea and wrote the proposal for the water development contract. Sure, I got a handshake or two when we won it, but guess who got put in charge of it when the work started? Right, old brownnose Farlow. Honey, I just can't wait till we get a little money set aside and we can drop out of this rat race. Just a little peace, that's what I need. Drinking is actually good for me right now. I don't think my nerves could take it if I didn't have something to calm me down at night. I can hardly unwind enough to get to sleep as it is."

Another really neat trick Denial uses is to redefine the problem so the drinker isn't included as part of it. One of his all-time favorites is the old "I can't be alcoholic because I still have my job, I've never been fired or reprimanded, and I just got a raise last week. Alcoholics can't hold down a job at all."

You'd be amazed at how much mileage is left in this old myth. The fact is, of course, that most alcoholics are employed, and most of them are considered satisfactory employees by their supervisors. Male alcoholics usually cling to this defense for years, since for men the job is usually the last thing to go.

A male alcoholic may have been through two or three or four marriages, a bankruptcy or two, and a handsome array of other personal problems, but that paycheck represents the ability to obtain an uninterrupted supply of liquor. There's just enough logic in the argument, however, and just enough myth and misinformation about alcoholism still floating around, to sell the "alcoholic can't hold a job" story to a lot of people.

The same story, with a different twist, applies to drug addicts and to alcoholics who combine booze with drugs. This tale goes: "I can't possibly be addicted. The doctor prescribed these pills. He said the pain would be unbearable if I stopped taking them." In other words, you can get as high as you want as often as you want, so long as the substance you're using is prescribed by a medical doctor or a psychiatrist.

Again, this argument carries considerable power, because as a society we respect doctors. Using the prescription gambit, Denial paves the way for thousands of chemically dependent people to continue using. Actually, prescription drugs can be every bit as addictive as street drugs or alcohol—or more—and they're almost as easy to get as alcohol.

Doctors receive little training in the effects of various drugs on alcoholics and other chemically dependent people, and they frequently do not fully understand the phenomenon of cross-addiction. In fact, many psychiatrists routinely prescribe drugs during therapy for a variety of disorders. As Dr. Joseph Pursch, best-known as the doctor who treated Betty Ford and Billy Carter, says in his film "The Life, Death, and Recovery of an Alcoholic," some psychiatrists prescribe drugs to alcoholics, apparently on the assumption that " . . . alcoholism is a Valium deficiency."

Once Denial gets this particular argument rolling, he can afford to sit back, relax, and enjoy the fun. I've seen Denial at work in treatment programs on a regular basis, as newly admitted patients minimize the severity of their respective dependencies.

Alcoholics, who may take a handful of pills on occasion to calm their nerves, nevertheless consider themselves superior to people who are so weak as to become addicted to a simple doctor's prescription. The pill-popper, meanwhile, is looking down his or her nose at the street drug folk, who will, he or she contends, put any substance into any available orifice, just to see what will happen. The street people accuse the prescription drug addicts of hypocrisy, since they use up to a dozen or so different doctors to obtain their drugs, then claim they can't be addicted because everything they take is legally prescribed. Older alcoholics go into an ethical rage about pot smokers, who have spent considerable energy denying that they're old enough to be addicted.

In treatment settings, the recognition that all the participants share a common, *single* disease, is frequently put aside while a debate filled with unfair accusations, bigotry, prejudice, bitterness, and ignorance rages. Unfortunately, most treatment specialists are trained in the art of breaking down Denial, so it's wise to stay away from those places at all costs.

Another common myth that still comes in handy is that beer or wine drinkers can't be alcoholic. Actually, each sixteen-ounce can of beer contains about the same amount of alcohol as a straight shot of whiskey. Drinking a six-pack in an hour is equal to downing six cocktails in an hour. Wine has an even higher alcohol content.

Beer alcoholics have an incredible capacity to down the stuff. It isn't uncommon for these folks to enter treatment programs with a two- or three-case-per-day habit.

Beer drinking also leaves you plenty of room for easy rationalization. For example, most beer drinkers can stall their critics by switching from five percent to 3.2 percent beer, or to one of the "light" brands.

Another trick of Denial's is to minimize the amount of alcohol used or the seriousness of the damage done. One of his favorite approaches is to point to other people and explain why those people have a far worse drinking problem than his own. Remember the fellow who drank lighter fluid only a couple of times? Denial was right there by his side, egging him on. Notice the skill with which this may be done, so that attention is diverted and the real problem minimized.

*　　*　　*

Let's say you're a married lady in your fifties whose husband is from the old school. His pride would be shattered if you had a career, so you've spent your adult life raising the children, cleaning house, and having dinner ready at 6:07 P.M. To cope with the boredom, you started having a little nip now and again.

As the children grew up, married and moved away, you became more lonely, and your bottle became an intimate friend. You can't wait for your husband to leave for work these days so you can renew your relationship with your friend. Being of the old school, it took your husband a long time to come right out and say something about your drinking. He noticed that the house wasn't quite as clean as before and that you weren't taking as much pride in your appearance, but he let it pass. Where you really screwed up was when you started having dinner at 6:10, 6:30, or sometimes not at all. Your husband has started to make some fairly direct comments about your drinking pattern. It's time to put out the call for good old Denial.

"Did you hear about poor Harry?" you ask casually over the spaghetti one evening. "He came home the other day and found Gladys gone. She'd packed up and left with that aluminum siding man she met down at Lefty's. I feel sorry for Harry. Everybody in town knew that Gladys was hanging around at Lefty's, letting anything in pants pick her up. He's probably better off now that she's gone."

You snuggle a bit closer to your husband, being careful not to breathe directly on him, and with a hint of Denial you say, "Dear, I know I take a little drink now and then. I miss you so much when you're gone. But I could never be the kind of person Gladys is. You know, I suspect that she's actually an alcoholic!"

*   *   *

I once witnessed a remarkable Hall of Fame performance by Denial. As far as I could tell, *all* of Denial's tricks were used during one episode by an alcoholic who had entered a treatment program after a wild binge involving his family, the police, several guns, and an impressive amount of bourbon. The guy had been through several detox centers and one or two treatment programs. Being a binge drinker, with the ability to go for weeks and months without touching a drop, he was able to fool people, including his own family, into thinking he had quit drinking permanently on a number of occasions.

In his moment of glory, the alcoholic was sitting among a circle of his family and treatment therapists in the dayroom of the center. He had his suitcase packed and had declared himself "cured" after about a week of treatment. The others were trying to talk him out of leaving.

"George," one therapist said, "remember the night they brought you in? That's happened a dozen or more times now. Don't you think it's time to admit you're an alcoholic and you need help?"

"Sure, I'm an alcoholic," George said. "And I did ask for help. That's why I came here."

"The cops brought you here," George's wife reminded.

"I would've come anyway," George said. "I just wanted to finish off that last bottle. They couldn't have forced me here if I had decided not to come."

"You were kicking and screaming and yelling," a therapist said.

"Well, they shouldn't have been pushing me. I would've come right along if they'd treated me right. At least I walked in on my own two feet. I wasn't drunk."

"They brought you down in a wheelchair," George's wife said.

"You had thrown up on yourself," a therapist said.

"I had done that the day before," George said.

"And your fly was unzipped. Do you usually go around in a wheelchair with your fly unzipped, wearing a shirt with yesterday's vomit on it, being restrained by two policemen who had been called to your house by neighbors because you were chasing your wife around with loaded guns?"

"It only happened once," George said.

Denial deserves an Oscar for that performance.

*　　*　　*

As strong as Denial is, even he gets tired and needs a break now and then. For most of us, we are eventually confronted by stupid or dangerous or simply unacceptable behavior that we can no longer deny. When this happens, we're forced to send Denial to the bench and try a different game plan.

Denial's first sub is usually an equally distinguished veteran named *Detour*. *Detour* has been around a long time. He can't play as many minutes as he could in his prime, but he can still be effective in spots.

Detour is more subtle than Denial in most respects. Where Denial uses brute strength to be effective, Detour tends to appeal to the mind. The basic difference between the two is that Denial comes right out and blames other people, places, and conditions for the alcoholic's behavior. Detour attempts to take attention away from alcoholism by *changing* the people, places, things and conditions involved. In other words, Denial says that drinking is not a problem, but that certain people, places, things, and conditions *are* problems and stops there. Detour, to be effective, must go a step further and admit that the person is, indeed, drinking too much. Detour's solution, however, is not to eliminate the drinking, but to change the "causes" that Denial identified and left hanging. Detour's arsenal, in addition to changing people, places, things, and conditions in our lives, includes such weapons as changing drinking or using patterns, changing the addiction or dependency, and even feigning the use of AA or treatment.

Detour usually is brought into the game on crucial downs only. Some crisis has probably occurred, and we have come up against what seems to be a rock and a hard place. It's fourth and forty on your own goal line, and the entire world knows you're going to have to punt. In other words, you're going to have to admit you're overdoing your drinking, you're going to have to get help, and you're going to have to cut down or stop. It appears inevitable. But the inevitable never stopped Detour.

"Okay, okay," Detour has you say. "I really blew it this time. My drinking caused a real problem. Tell you what. I'll switch from Jack Daniels to beer, and I'll drink only on weekends. That'll take care of everything, I promise."

Not only will this work, but variations of the same theme will work time after time. The second variation could be, "I'll go on the wagon for an entire month." A third: "Okay, this is it. Two beers a day and no more. You must admit, it really helped to switch to beer. But you know how nervous I am. I need a little something to relax me every day. I just get too uptight if I have to wait until the weekend. I can handle a couple of beers a day. No sweat."

Detour also works through methods such as taking a trip: "We're just overtired and overworked. Let's take that month off in the mountains and get ourselves together again. Have you seen the cooler?"

This kind of vacation trip or temporary scenic reprieve from reality may lead, in time, to a Detour tactic that veteran recovering alcoholics call the "geographic escape." Though used by practically every alcoholic who has had reason to call on Detour, this ploy still works. In its simplest form, the geographic escape consists of convincing your family that where you live is responsible for the way you drink (if you live in the country, the isolation drives you to drink; if you live in the city, the constant hustle-bustle drives you to drink). The solution to your drinking, you declare, is to move someplace else. You never stop drinking, of course, but you can usually accomplish a cross-county relocation or two before your trusting brood catches on.

You can use Detour in the same manner to claim that changing jobs will solve your drinking problem, or that hanging out with a bunch of new friends will do the trick. The ultimate Detour, and one that many alcoholics use, is changing spouses. That seems to be the magic cure, particularly if your new spouse drinks as much as you do.

Some alcoholics don't drink so much when they're busy, so another Detour technique is to become a workaholic. This doesn't do much for the family life, but it may help the finances for a time. And when the kids answer the phone, they usually know it's Dad or Mom saying they have to work late, not a request to bring bail money to the police station. This, too, is only a temporary diversionary tactic. Only in extreme cases does work replace alcohol on a permanent basis. A return to your typical drinking is almost assured, especially when job pressure becomes great.

In the same tradition, food can become a temporary Detour, since many alcoholics don't like to drink on a full stomach. This is usually a temporary fancy, with the only result being a massive weight gain from the combined caloric increase of food and booze. We've already discussed substituting pills for alcohol, which is a frequent indicator that Detour is hard at work.

Experienced as he is, even Detour—like Denial before him—has a breaking point. There comes a time when the determined alcoholic has exhausted all of Detour's many talents. The last gasp usually comes when Detour is using AA and treatment as methods to preserve alcoholic drinking. If this doesn't make sense, you've underestimated both Detour and the determination of most of us to continue drinking.

What happens, you see, is that after everybody has caught on to the fact that none of Detour's tricks has relieved our drinking or our problems, we're once again between the rock and the hard place. It's almost time to punt. But not quite. Detour may suggest that we actually start attending AA or enter a treatment program, and we may indeed follow through. But that doesn't mean we've given up on drinking. It simply means that we can go to these places to prove that they don't work. Some of the grandest drinking sprees I've ever seen have taken place between the time an alcoholic left an AA meeting and reached home, or within an hour after he or she has walked out of treatment.

Our second D, Detour, is pooped. It's time to bring on the third D, *Delay*, fresh, rested, and ready for action.

*   *   *

Delay's effectiveness lies in his deceptiveness. He's a master of camouflage. To the sober world, he appears to be a sigh of relief, an answer to prayers, a breath of fresh air. Delay's first words are: "I am an alcoholic. I can't control my drinking. I want to change. I need help." That's music to his loved ones' ears. Unfortunately for them, they're usually listening to the music so avidly they miss Delay's true message: "*But not yet!*" See, Delay hasn't sold you out.

The primary difference between Detour and Delay is that Detour had no intention of tackling the real problem. Delay is more honest, if not totally so. He realizes that the problem is drinking, that drinking has been pegged as the problem, and that something is going to have to be done specifically about drinking. But time can be bought to postpone the actual biting of the bullet.

Delay's sell is so soft that the alcoholic's loved ones will actually believe and participate in the most outlandishly illogical schemes one can imagine. Example: "Sweetheart, I've admitted that my drinking is out of control and I have to have help. In fact, my drinking has caused such problems between us that I think we should start going to a marriage counselor right away." Happily, sweetheart agrees.

We alcoholics see exactly what has been accomplished. We've managed to convince our loved one that we're doing something about our drinking without actually doing anything about our drinking. In fact, we're putting at least half the burden on the spouse, since marriage counseling (if we play our cards right and pick a counselor who is not knowledgeable about alcoholism) will give us enough stuff to work on and fight about for several years. Sometimes Delay is so smooth that he can convince the nondrinking spouse that it would be better not to confuse the issue by bringing alcoholism into the conversation with the marriage counselor.

I saw Delay in action for more than five years with one couple. The guy—all the while admitting that his drinking was out of control and professing that he was in desperate need of help—went to a psychiatrist (who prescribed Valium), then to a social worker (who gave him some family exercises to work on), to a minister (who told him to come to church regularly and to pray a lot), to a vocational counselor (who enrolled him in a truck driving school until the guy got a DWI and lost his license), back to the psychiatrist (who tried a different pill this time), and around the circle again; the wife was still facing all the problems her husband's active alcoholism was presenting (complicated now by prescription drugs), but she was letting her husband enjoy his disease in peace.

"After all," she told her friends, "he's trying as hard as he can to stay sober."

One day at Al-Anon a lady asked the wife, "Why hasn't your husband ever talked to an AA member who is recovering, or gone to a treatment program? If he really wants to recover from alcoholism, why is it he never talks to anybody who specializes in it?"

Delay's cover was blown right then and there, and the poor guy eventually entered treatment and gave up drinking.

But being forced into AA or a treatment program isn't the end. Delay even has a number of tricks to help you sabotage recovery. We'll refer back to these things from time to time so you can pick up specific pointers.

5

Developing Your Personality

Most people haven't spent a lot of time thinking about what goes into personality. Actually, if you sliced a personality open, you would find that it doesn't contain as much stuff as you may have supposed. All you'll find are a few things that make us react to and interact with other people and with our environment. It's how we use this machinery that determines what kind of personality we have.

Alcoholics, contrary to the opinion of many people who live and work with us, don't have personality traits that other people don't have. We just display our traits differently. These traits are not good or bad of themselves, but they may be helpful or destructive, depending on how we use them.

No matter how much we pretend to the contrary, our personality characteristics did not cause us to drink. We did not become alcoholic because we're naturally dependent, because we were rebellious as children, or because our mothers made us wax the kitchen floor every half-hour. We can blame these things for our drinking, and, fortunately for us, many people will believe it. But it just isn't so.

For years, I said I became an alcoholic because I was always a sensitive person, and my friends and family would nod and say, "Yes, indeed he is." It apparently never occurred to anyone that the world is literally filled with sensitive people who did not become alcoholics.

Sensitive or not, dramatic personality changes can —and do—take place in anyone when alcohol or other chemicals are introduced.

Without doubt, the prolonged use of alcohol and other chemicals alters the personality in a way that often leads to problems. For example, when we require alcohol in regular doses to function, we are forced to develop ways of acting and reacting that protect our right to drink. As a result, we discover how to manipulate our thoughts to justify and protect our need and our right to exist as drinkers. That's a fascinating personality trait right there.

As the years pass, our ways of acting and reacting become more and more ingrained. Most people tend to become a bit set in their ways as time passes, whether they're alcoholic or not, but remember—what makes us special is that our ingrained personality traits are altered or distorted by drinking, and so this tends to cause us problems.

Another special thing about our personalities is that we may continue our distorted, problem-causing patterns even during periods when we aren't drinking. This factor also serves as a type of guarantee that we will always return to drinking, since we'll continue to run into problems, and the way we've learned to deal with problems is to drink. So, we have ourselves set up in a nice little cycle supportive of our drinking. This is a primary reason, incidentally, why drying out, or a few days of detoxification, rarely results in permanent sobriety. The body may be dry, but the personality is still drunk, so to speak.

The types of problems our alcoholic personalities create are wide-ranging and impressive.

We tend not to tolerate frustration very well. We're impatient, we're easily irritated, and we're opinionated.

Patience is not a major virtue for many people, but we have turned impatience into an art form. We'll procrastinate for days and weeks and months, but when we decide we want something, we want it immediately.

We can also play a lot of games with the fact that we become irritated—frequently, thoroughly, and especially with spouses and children. We're like sharks; if you don't irritate us, we'll leave you alone. The problem our families face is trying to figure out what irritates a shark. If they stood back and studied the situation with detachment, they'd probably decide simply to stay out of the water and not play the game. We're so skilled, however, that we probably wouldn't let them get away with it. We'd crawl up on the beach and drag them in. There's usually no need to go to such extremes, though. People close to us seem compelled to jump right in and accept our rules of competition. Al-Anon calls these people "enablers," who through their good intentions make it easier for us to drink. God bless them.

Another way our low tolerance for frustration surfaces is in our tendency to become more opinionated the longer we drink. One advantage to being opinionated is that we don't have to defend our ideas very often. After a few friendly attempts, some people will go out of their way not to talk to us, while others will agree with anything we say just so they don't have to be subjected to an hour-long discourse in their area of expertise.

*   *   *

Anxiety is one of our more useful alcoholic personality traits, since we can use it in a variety of ways. The most obvious, of course, is that we can present it to many medical doctors or psychiatrists and trade it in for a couple years' worth of prescription drugs, which we can combine with booze or use to sustain ourselves during those periods when we're proving to our spouses that we don't need to have a drink.

The effectiveness of anxiety is enhanced by the fact that it is very real. In its most common form, it confronts us as a free-floating sense of dread and apprehension. It hangs around even when everything seems to be going our way. The bills are all paid for once, the spouse hasn't complained about our drinking for an entire week (he or she has been going to Al-Anon), and two full fifths are stashed away in our emergency hiding place. All should be right with the world. But it isn't.

We feel a sense of doom, we feel guilty, and we're worried. In fact, we feel so guilty and worried that we break out one of the fifths to settle our nerves. Our spouses catch us but don't say anything, and that irritates us. We become so irritated, in fact, that we get drunk and find something to confront them about, so that they will wipe that smug look off their faces. We eventually succeed. She flees to the bedroom in tears or he storms out of the house. We take a long swig, look up at the ceiling, and spy our old friend, free-floating anxiety, hovering up there.

The only difference now is that we have something specific to feel anxious about. Guilt and worry set in again, so we fetch the other emergency fifth. We should be grateful for anxiety. See what it can do for us?

Grandiosity is one of my favorite alcoholic personality traits. It helps us put on a great show when the mood is right. In periods of effective grandiosity, we command the center of attention. We brag about our achievements (whether or not they've actually been achieved), we dramatize the events in our lives, and we monopolize conversations. We swagger, we overdress, we try to seduce anything that resembles a human being. We have the best material possessions, the worst problems, and the answer to every eternal question ever posed.

Our most outstanding periods of grandiosity often coincide with payday. Because of our penchant for blowing an entire paycheck in a couple of hours, bartenders call this trait the "Set 'em up, Joe" syndrome. One of my recovering friends observed that on these occasions, bars usually are filled only with well-heeled boozers. "There are no unemployed ditch-diggers in bars on payday," he said. How true. We may as well reach for the gusto while we can, because payday is as fleeting as its rewards.

I suppose all of us realize that the true feeling underlying grandiosity is one of inadequacy. Those of us who possess this trait are often fearful that people won't like or respect us as we really are, so we try to impress them by embellishing our real achievements, creating other achievements, spending money we can't afford, and behaving in a generally boorish manner. Chances are, many nonalcoholics who know us would laugh in our faces if they found out we were behaving that way because we feel insecure and incompetent. Our show of superiority is a painful charade.

But we know how to deal with pain, don't we? Reality returns soon enough; why force it?

"Set 'em up again, Joe."

*   *   *

Several of my friends have achieved solid drinking careers by relying primarily on one distorted personality trait—perfectionism. The way this works is that the person sets goals which are unrealistically high for himself or herself and for others, avoids anything he or she can't do perfectly, and feels guilty and worthless when those goals prove to be unreachable. And, please respond in unison, what do we do when we feel guilty and worthless? Right. We drink.

I know an alcoholic woman who is so perfectionistic about her house that it always looks like a pigpen. Her goal, obviously, is to have a one hundred percent clean, beautiful, spotless house at all times. With four kids, a dog, a cat, and a construction-worker husband running in and out, her goal is clearly unrealistic. Since she can't achieve this goal, she does as little housework as possible, saying, "If I can't do things right, I won't do them at all." She justifies a fifth-a-day habit with no sweat whatsoever.

$$* \quad * \quad *$$

Wishful thinking has kept thousands of alcoholics going. These lucky people live in a fantasy world, in which their big break is always just around the corner. They're convinced that all their problems will be solved by a once-in-a-lifetime stroke of luck. I once survived for six months in Washington, D.C., convinced that my financial problems would be solved by winning a weekly newspaper puzzle. I didn't try to budget my money or pay off any creditors because I knew it was just a matter of time until I hit the jackpot. The odds against winning, incidentally, were something like 160,000 to one.

An important part of wishful thinking is the ability to alter reality to fit the way we think it should be. With this skill, we are able to transform an alcohol-influenced business disaster into a case of sheer bad luck. Or a missed promotion into the boss's bad judgment. We are able to disassociate entirely from the fact that our financial hardships may be at least partially attributable to the expenditure of several hundred (or thousand, in some cases) dollars for weekly booze and booze-related activities.

Wishful thinking can be pleasant, particularly when we have a couple of drinks along with it. Unfortunately, we usually end up wishing we had been doing something constructive with the time we spent in wishful thinking.

*   *   *

Probably no other personality trait so enhances the alcoholic's commitment to drinking as a sense of being alone, even when he or she is among other people. We tend to isolate ourselves from others when this trait is active, but we've learned that the bottle is always reliable company.

Some alcoholics are exceptionally gifted at achieving and using isolation to further their drinking. It isn't uncommon at all for us to feel that we don't belong anyplace. Some alcoholics, for example, feel so alienated from everyone, including their own families, that they brood in a lonely room for hours about whether they're adopted. I know a few alcoholics who have actually had blood tests to verify their parents' stories.

A creative variation on this theme is to conclude that we're different because we're better. We're more intelligent than other people, or we travel a different and more challenging path. A touch of grandiosity frequently appears at this point.

In the last analysis, isolation (with a good supply of your favorite brand) is a perfect solution to a whole raft of social problems. Haven't we spent hours telling ourselves—and others—that we don't need other people anyway?

*   *   *

Almost all alcoholics, at least the ones I know, are proud of their sensitivity. Even the people most frustrated by our alcoholic behavior usually grant us a high degree of this personality trait. With such support, is it any wonder that we can turn sensitivity into an outstanding rationalization for continued drinking? And sell this idea to ourselves and others?

With a little practice, we can become so supersensitive that our behavior may either border on, or cross over into, paranoia. Typically, the most innocent, everyday, off-the-cuff remark can set the stage for a marvelous week-long binge. When we enter a room and see a group of people talking in soft voices, we may "logically" conclude that they're talking about us. And, depending on how much we've had to drink and how we've behaved, they may indeed be talking about us, with good reason.

Or when the boss smiles at us in the elevator and says, "I'm hearing good things about your department," we wonder exactly what he meant. Somehow we manage to feel misunderstood. And we are.

*   *   *

Probably the most typical alcoholic personality trait is impulsiveness. Routines bore us, so we do things on impulse. Early on, this can be an endearing, fresh quality. Unfortunately, it may tend to wear a bit thin as our impulsive behavior progresses into some pretty crazy things. If you need proof of this point, spend a drunken evening listening to your equally drunken friends tell of the trips they've taken from coast to coast on impulse, and the disasters they've endured in the process.

Impulsiveness prevents us from enjoying any kind of planning. We want to spring right into the action. We don't have any long-term goals because we can't wait for tomorrow (impatience can team up very logically here), and we tend to do things in a mad dash.

We want to get a job done as quickly as possible, but we don't get our jollies from the actual doing of the task. When we cut the lawn, for example, we're so busy plotting out how much ground we need to cover before we can justify a beer break that the smell and feel of nature don't really affect us.

We also tend to start a lot of projects and finish very few of them, because after the newness wears off, the job becomes boring. According to recovering people, alcoholics believe that inspiration is better than perspiration.

*   *   *

Nobody is better at being defiant than alcoholics. We rival three-year-olds in our ability to rebel at the smallest thing, and we become extremely skilled at knowing how and when to throw tantrums for their greatest effect. Recovering alcoholics contend that there's a good reason why we can emulate childish behavior so well. They say that we stopped growing emotionally when alcohol took control of our lives. In fact, it isn't unusual to hear AA members in their thirties, forties, fifties and older talk about having an "emotional age" of eighteen or twenty, or whatever age they began drinking alcoholically.

Behavioral psychologists could write a book or two about this, but we alcoholics probably wouldn't have the patience to read them. We have, remember, a low tolerance for things we don't understand and for people who claim to know more than we do.

*   *   *

In usable terms, we can exploit our defiance (and our other distorted personality traits) because we have succeeded in deadening our emotional responses to other people's feelings and to social propriety.

We don't care what other people think or feel, so long as we get our way. And, like the three-year-old, if our tantrum is most effective when it's thrown in a situation which is potentially embarrassing to our target (like the child in the grocery store screaming for candy), that's exactly where we'll throw it. We have a built-in, self-protection mechanism to shield us from the consequences of emotional improprieties. When our consciences start bothering us or we start feeling guilty, all we need is more alcohol or another pill or twelve and our emotions are shoved back into the corner.

Defiance is a valuable tool for us. Through its use, we can honestly say such things as, "I've never had a wife (or husband or girlfriend or boyfriend) leave me because of my drinking." This could be absolutely true: maybe *we've* always left *them*. Defiance allows us to see the handwriting on the wall and reject other people before they throw up their hands in exasperation and reject us. We can use the same argument in a variety of situations: "I can't be an alcoholic because I've never been fired from a job." That may be true, and we see no need to add that we have quit fifteen jobs in the past three years because people in each situation began to comment about our absenteeism or drinking lunches.

The most creative defiance I ever observed was used by a prim and proper lady who was forced into treatment by her husband and her children.

"I quit my last two jobs," she said, quite self-righteously, "because everybody drank at work. I never drank until after work." She didn't drink on the job, but she failed to show up for work on Monday mornings more than eighty percent of the time.

Like many alcoholic personality traits, defiance can be perceived as a positive quality. We may receive positive strokes for rebelling against society's wrongs, for having the courage to speak our convictions regardless of the consequences, or for being our "own person." If we could stop the personality progression right there, alcoholics might go down in history next to Nathan Hale as champions of right and morality. Unfortunately, we ultimately show our rebellious nature against people and events which, rationally, do not qualify as great causes. Quitting a job because the janitor always puts the toilet paper on the dispenser backwards, for example, is not the stuff from which greatness evolves.

The defiance in our personalities requires that we not tolerate direct orders. In fact, we cannot long endure a situation in which we're given directions. It makes no difference that the directions may be correct, or that we don't know how to proceed without them. The mere fact that they are being given is sufficient grounds to rebel.

Here's a typical defiant alcoholic on the job:

Boss: Jones, we need that stack of plimments moved two feet to the left. Could you have it done by quitting time?

Jones: What's wrong with it right there?

Boss: It's in the way of the new shipment of grummels that's coming in first thing in the morning.

Jones: Who the hell ordered grummels? We haven't sold any for two months.

Boss: They're pre-sold. Let me know if you need help.

Jones: (*Later, in bar, to coworker Smith*) Geez, you'd think he's the only guy in the whole company who knows anything. I don't mind doing the work, but it was the way he said it.

Smith: Maybe he's got it in for you. He's never treated me that way.

Jones: I think he's jealous. He knows I stand up for myself and he's just a puppet of the home office. He lets himself get pushed around and he tries to take it out on me. Well, he's got another thing coming if he thinks he can take out his insecurities on me. Let's have another round.

Smith: We've already had six. I've got to get home. The kids will be waiting for me.

Jones: I don't want to go home feeling like this. No use taking the job out on the family. In fact, I think my family would get along a whole lot better if I just walked away from the job.

Smith: Yeah. So long.

The next morning:

Boss: (*To Smith*) Have you seen Jones? He was supposed to have that stack of plimments moved. The truck with the grummels is already here. Would you move it? And if Jones shows up, tell him I want to see him.

Jones: (*Upon arriving late, to Smith*) What the devil are you doing my job for? I said I would do it. Are you trying to get in good with the boss?

Smith: Nope. Just had to get this stuff out of the way.
            The boss wants to see you.

Jones: Guess he never came to work with a hangover.
            You tell him I quit, will you? I'll be at Rosie's if
            you want a cold one after work. And pick up my
            severance pay. We'll celebrate my freedom.

Defiance doesn't always work so quickly or so directly, but it is a favorite alcoholic ploy. Since we can't tolerate direct orders, we can rely upon our defiance to avoid the real issues. We can procrastinate, we can ignore orders, or, if we please, we can sabotage the honest efforts of other people.

Sabotage is perhaps the meanest trick an alcolholic —or anyone else, for that matter—can use. If someone else's reputation depends partly on us, we can do less than our best and let the other person take the heat. Through subtle manipulation in a job situation, we can make our supervisor look so incompetent that we can take his place. This may sound wonderful to a practicing alcoholic, but it usually backfires. Too often, our primary ability has been to make someone else look bad, and we may not have the skills—much less the inclination—to do the other person's job. It may interfere with our drinking.

Dependency is another personality trait that goes hog-wild for the typical alcoholic. It's deceptive, in that most alcoholics pride themselves on being independent, and most people who live with alcoholics mistake dependency for arrogance or some other clever cover-up.

In truth, we often tend to be dependent to an extreme. Regardless of our periodic shows of bravado and defiance (always, you'll notice, with a fifth or two of courage under our belts), we desperately want to live up to the expectations of others. We'll say what we think others want to hear rather than express our real feelings. We'll become what we think other people want us to be, even when that may not be what we want for ourselves. We are, in short, people-pleasers. We also have very little belief in our own convictions. We're afraid to make decisions for ourselves, and we let other people do for us what we're afraid to do for ourselves.

"Whoa," you may say, quite understandably, "just tell me how Jones, in your little story, was a dependent, indecisive, people-pleasing wimp?"

Upon close examination, you'll notice that Jones only talked a good game. When it came down to the crunch, he asked Smith to tell the boss that he quit, and he imposed on Smith's friendship to avoid showing up at the payroll office to get his final check. Jones was even using Smith to avoid going home and talking over the real problem with his family. He was trying to please Smith by appearing to reveal his feelings (we usually feel closer to people when it seems that they're letting us catch a glimpse of their true selves). He was even trying to please his wife by protecting his image of a hard-working breadwinner who was up against a brick wall not of his own making.

In reality, Jones's use of defiance and his manipulation of his dependencies were geared toward one thing: the protection of his drinking. He may have thought he loved his wife and kids, but his behavior showed his primary love affair—with the bottle.

One does not have to go beyond Psychology 101 (if that far) to hang the appropriate tag on the behavior of a people-pleaser: passive-aggressiveness. The person allows himself or herself to be imposed upon, and then expends the resulting anger in a way that may have no relation to the event that caused the anger.

Passive-aggressive behavior should not be a great concern for us drinkers. Our spouses and other family members, because they choose to object to our drinking and can't handle their own irrationality, are the ones who develop this pattern to a high degree. They often become so obviously passive-aggressive, in fact, that we may be tempted to invite friends over, let them look at our loved ones, shake our heads sadly and say, "See? That's why I drink."

But seriously, folks, the reason we may engage in passive-aggressive behavior without worrying too much about it is that we know a friend when we see one. We know that if we suppress our anger we will begin to resent the people who—at least in our opinion—caused the anger. Then, the resentment will lead to drinking, which will lead to the reinforcement of our passive-aggressive activities, which will lead to drinking, *ad infinitum.*

*　　*　　*

It should be clear that maintaining our unique personality traits, however distorted they may appear to be, is vital if we are to continue to drink in the manner to which we have become accustomed. So, in order to continue drinking, beware of change.

First, in order to change anything, including a personality trait, it must be identified. This can mean either not listening at all to what other people say they see in us, or listening to what they have to say so we can apply that information to the construction of a better defense.

Another way personality problems may be eliminated is by discovering the honest feelings that underlie the various characteristics. For example, if lashing out in anger is one of your typical personality characteristics, you should continue to focus other people's attention on your anger. What you're really feeling, of course, is more likely to be fear than anger. And that must be disguised at all times.

I've seen some hard cases cracked when the alcoholic allowed someone to discover this fact. Once a counselor or a therapist puts the finger on fear as the true emotion, even the strongest alcoholic is likely to break down and blubber like a baby.

Other true feelings may be: fear vs. perfectionism (I'm afraid I won't be as good as I'm expected to be); inadequacy vs. isolation (I'm afraid they'll see me as I really am); emotional hurt vs. defiance (I'll not ask her out for next Saturday night if she won't go tonight); or rejection vs. dependency (if I don't keep dinner warm until he's ready to eat, he'll find someone else).

As I've said, we don't possess personality traits radically different from those of other people. And these traits are not good or bad of themselves. It's just how we use them as reasons, excuses, and justifications for drinking.

6

Maintaining the Proper Attitude

If, as they say, attitudes shape the person, we drinkers are in a class by ourselves. Our attitudes are usually as deep-seated as our desire to drink. And since the popular belief is that a person is incapable of changing certain attitudes, the alcoholic can logically claim: "I may be wrong, but that's the way I look at things. That's the way my father looked at things, and that's the way his father looked at things. You can't teach an old dog new tricks."

*   *   *

We pick up attitudes throughout our lives, just like wrinkles and gray hair. Our first attitudes are learned at a very young age. We receive them from our parents and the rest of our family. To prove a point about attitudes, you can put young children of different races or religions together, and they may become good buddies. They have yet to learn that their basic values of equality and friendship aren't widely held by society. They'll absorb that attitude as they grow older.

We pick up some attitudes from religion, and a whole bundle as we go through school. We begin to take shape as adults who will think, feel and act upon the attitudes held by the majority of our community. Life will probably proceed smoothly, attitude-wise, until we run into some situations that simply won't fit into the neat little boxes we'd prepared for every occasion. When this happens, we find ourselves face-to-face with a contradiction, which brings with it a built-in excuse to drink.

* * *

Most of our attitude changes occur when we encounter a contradiction between life experiences and the attitude we happen to hold at the moment of contradiction.

Typical contradictions may include such a mundane thing as: "My parents told me that men are mechanically inclined, but I can't fix anything."

Many young mothers, I'm told, have a few things to say to their own mothers when they discover that the word "pain" was somehow left out of the descriptions about the joyous experience of childbirth.

As young adults, we may develop a different attitude toward responsibility when we get our first car and are told we have to pay for it and maintain it. Our attitudes toward marriage and being a parent usually change as those events happen to us. Our first experience with death, divorce and financial difficulty may dictate extreme attitudinal revision.

* * *

A contradiction that has profound impact on heavy drinkers involves the way alcohol and drugs were presented to them as young people. Until quite recently, schools and churches (and many parents) prepared their young charges to avoid the evils of chemicals by scaring the daylights out of them.

One sip of beer, they were led to believe, would lead to a life in the town gutter.

A drag from a marijuana cigarette would be followed almost immediately by total dependence on heroin.

It should have been obvious that these attitudes would never stick. Regardless of the sincerity and motivation of the instructors, the adolescent will almost certainly encounter contradictions between what people say and the realities they encounter.

When the first actual experience with alcohol or drugs comes, the teachings of the elders are usually laid to rest. One can, indeed, drink a beer (or even several) and find the world the next morning pretty much the same as it was the night before.

*　　*　　*

The contradictions between what we're told about heavy drinking or alcoholism and what actually happens may continue for years. We're told alcoholics lose their families, but in most cases, it takes a long time before that happens. Until it does, we alcoholics merely add one more excuse to our repertoire: "I'm not an alcoholic because I still have my family." We sometimes go through three or four or more families before we finally own up to the fact that alcohol might have something to do with our inability to hang on to our marriage. Even then, losing one's family is but one of dozens of so-called symptoms, many of which we insist on experiencing for ourselves.

Other widely held attitudes help us keep on drinking as we please. The old attitude that one cannot become alcoholic by drinking beer, for example, provides much confusion and even more grounds for rationalization. But our greatest refuge may be in the attitude that a person must be on skid row to be a real alcoholic. More than ninety-five percent of us alcoholics are self-supporting folks who represent both sexes, all ages, races and religions, and who range from blue-collar workers to corporate executives. Most AA meetings resemble a demographic slice of normal, decent Americana, believe it or not.

*　　*　　*

A logical result of contradiction is confusion, and there are two things we can do about it. We can resolve the contradictions that led to the confusion and get on with our lives, or we may leave the contradictions unresolved and try to find some way (hint, hint) to cope with the confusion.

For the person who is committed to drinking, these contradictions must remain unresolved. This isn't to say that we simply ignore them—quite the contrary. We can find ways to bring them to the fore to cloud almost any issue, and detract attention from our right to drink.

The good Lord doubly blessed the alcoholic when He provided for these contradictions to abound in our lives. As we drink to deal with contradictions and the ensuing confusion, things become more confusing and more contradictory, thereby requiring more drinking.

I grew up in a fundamentalist Christian church where drinking was considered a sin. Yet I saw a church deacon soused to the gills almost every night of the week. Nobody said anything about the deacon's drinking, and when the preacher assured us that a sip of wine would send us straight to hell, the good deacon sat in the front pew alternately nodding off and emitting a holy "Amen!" at appropriate intervals. I didn't ask the preacher, even in private, if the deacon was going to hell. Instead, I let it ride, and a contradiction that would help shape my attitude about drinking took root. As a budding alcoholic, I could now rationalize any type of drinking and expect to escape responsibility for any consequences. Hallelujah.

*   *   *

There's one other attitude I'd like to share with you, if you're really serious about protecting your drinking. And I assume you are. It involves Alcoholics Anonymous. Many people, including some of us drinkers, tend to view AA with a bit of awe and reverence.

If you find yourself thinking and feeling this way, watch out—you're harboring an attitude that can get you sober. What to do about it? Simple. Take a good, honest look at AA. What is it, after all? It's a bunch of drunks and former drunks, that's what—people who don't have enough will power to quit drinking on their own. AA meetings can be boring and depressing. People sit around in poorly lit rooms, sip coffee, and talk about their failures. Even worse, they talk about even their small successes.

Most of the people who go to AA don't have two nickles to rub together. Actually, that's probably the only reason they go to meetings; they don't have enough money to go to the bar. Some, of course, do both. You don't have to look very hard to find a few folks who head directly for the nearest watering hole as soon as the Serenity Prayer is finished at the end of the meeting.

People at AA are even more hypocritical and blasphemous than people who go to church. They curse, swap lurid stories about their sexual escapades and brushes with the law, and then—in the same breath—talk about a close relationship with their Higher Power.

It's enough to drive a person to drink.

*   *   *

If the sins listed above weren't enough, AA also has a penchant for trite little phrases. You may have noticed that. They even have a cute saying for unresolved contradictions: Stinkin' thinkin'. Stinkin' thinkin' involves supposedly irrational attitudes which drinkers perfect and apply. Of course, AA's idea is that we should take these attitudes, see how wrong they are, and change them into positive attitudes. Let's take a look at the list:

Stinkin' Thinkin'

1. Making mistakes is terrible.

2. People should be condemned for their wrong-doings.

3. My emotions can't be controlled.

4. People must love and approve of me.

5. Threatening situations have to keep me worried.

6. Self-discipline is too hard to achieve.

7. Bad effects of my childhood still have to control my life.

8. I can't stand the way certain people act.

9. People should act the way I think is right.

10. I'm responsible for making everybody else happy.

As you can see, following any or all of these ten beliefs would drive anyone to drink. Not only do irrational attitudes add determination to our drinking, we can master them to the point that we can make other people consider turning to drink.

For example, my wife comes home and wants to know where the rent money is. She's carrying an eviction notice the landlord just hand-delivered. We have twenty-four hours to either pay in full or pack up and leave. Since I was playing "Set 'em up, Joe" at the bar all afternoon, I obviously don't have any money left for rent. Or for groceries, for that matter.

Normally, I would skulk off somewhere while my wife figured out how to extricate us from this latest crisis. Now, however, armed with my Stinkin' Thinkin' list, I can say, "Do you know what your problem is? Every time you run into a little snag, you worry it to death. Don't you know that threatening situations don't have to keep you worried all the time? And so what if I spent all the money? You shouldn't always condemn other people for their wrongdoings. You think everybody should act the way you think is right. There you go, crying again. You seem to think your emotions can't be controlled. Anytime a person doesn't love and approve everything you do, you fall to pieces. Honestly, sometimes I think I'm responsible for making everybody in the world happy. You'd better start packing, while I go down to the bar to figure out how to deal with this mess." Nifty little gadgets, those irrational beliefs. No need to change them at all—if you want to keep on drinking.

*   *   *

There are some attitudes we need to stay away from if we are to continue our drinking. We must try not to think of ourselves as having the ability to change ourselves for the better. We must never admit, even in the privacy of our own thoughts, that we are responsible for our individual success. After all, which of us would want to think that we're accountable for the messes we've gotten into? And we must be uniformly unforgiving when we make a mistake. When we're wrong, we must react as though the sky were falling. And consume massive quantities of alcohol in order to live with ourselves.

We must also avoid positive attitudes about other people. We can't give up the attitude that other people, places and conditions control us, or that their intentions for us are sinister.

We should avoid ever admitting we need help, but if we're forced into that trap, we should close ourselves off from accepting it. If, for example, we continue drinking after attending several AA meetings or participating in a treatment program, we should say, "See? AA didn't help me." Or, "Treatment didn't make me well. What's the use?"

The list is endless.

7

Casting Out Spiritual Beliefs

Alcoholism is said to be a disease of the mind, body and spirit. We've talked about the mind and body, so all that's left is the spirit—whatever that is. Few people understand the spiritual nature of alcoholism, but, unfortunately, those who claim to are fanatical about it. So a word to the wise: If someone starts talking to you about spirituality in relation to your drinking, you've more than likely encountered yet another of the million or so AA and Al-Anon members who inhabit the earth.

AA teaches that to become permanently and comfortably sober, one must recover spiritually. To become spiritually healthy, according to AA, a person must learn to talk about spirituality intelligently and in a non-threatening manner. That, of course, is a tall order for anyone short of sainthood. So there's not much for us to worry about in this area. It requires very little effort or ingenuity on our part to sabotage discussions about spirituality. A few shouting matches or displays of injured feelings can discourage all but the stouthearted from discussing spirituality with us.

Still, we need to discuss what is meant by spirituality, which, in the AA vernacular, is quite distinct from religion.

*   *   *

Religion may be defined as a system of faith or belief that is shared with others. When we talk about religion, we usually imply the existence of a specific building or place of worship: a church, a cathedral, a synagogue, a temple.

Another thing religions usually have is dogma. The word "dogma" has come to have a somewhat negative connotation, as it implies rigidity and unreasonableness, as in a "dogmatic" person. Actually, all it means is that a religion has a definite theological belief system. Baptism by immersion, for example, is the dogma of several Christian denominations, while sprinkling holy water for baptism is accepted dogma among others.

While it is difficult—and perhaps a bit unfair—to attempt to categorize religions, it is probably safe to say that religions are, by and large, organizations for people who hold relatively compatible views about religious and spiritual matters. Religions also provide the place and the forum for the further study of these matters, and for the sharing of beliefs and insights.

*   *   *

Spirituality, as opposed to religion, involves an individual's personal belief system. This system may or may not coincide with the dogma of a religion. Spirituality has to do with the one-on-one relationship a person has with a "Higher Power." It involves one's own values and how one's behavior conforms to these values. It concerns how we see ourselves in the world, in relation to our Higher Power (which we may or may not refer to as God), and whether or not we see meaning and a purpose in life. Our spirituality also seems to have great influence on whether we see life from a generally positive or a generally negative perspective. A willingness to listen to other people and the ability to respect their opinions are major parts of the package marked "spirituality."

Spirituality is something that takes place inside the person. It is a highly personal quality, unique to each individual. For this reason, recovering people who are working what AA calls a "good program" do not insist that others cannot recover equally well, even though their concepts of spirituality and God may differ. This doesn't mean that recovering alcoholics sit back and say nothing about God, the Higher Power, religion, and spirituality. In fact, some will talk at great length about how they discovered their Higher Power, how their spiritual beliefs contribute to their sobriety, and how their spiritual insights may be shared with others.

You may notice, however, that certain phrases are missing from the recovering person's vocabulary, phrases such as: "This is how God works," or "You have to believe such and such if your Higher Power is to help you." The recovering person may listen to someone else say, "My Higher Power lives in a phone booth and gives crackers to orphaned parrots," and never bat an eyelash.

You, of course, can carefully record such nonsensical references, and use them to ridicule the philosophy of AA and its members. Such pearls of AA drivel play well in bars and in exchanges with would-be reformers.

The other aspects of spirituality that set it apart from religion include the belief that each individual is free to grow and change spiritually as he or she experiences life, and that each individual is free to choose a God, or Higher Power, of his or her understanding.

Fortunately for us drinkers, understanding how religion and spirituality differ and how their respective, legitimate roles affect our lives is a matter for great discussion and debate. And if you're skilled in such matters, you can usually develop an ironclad defense for rejecting

AA and all it stands for. AA simply wouldn't exist without its spiritual underpinnings.

*   *   *

Despite all kinds of shadings and degrees of belief, there are three basic stances about God that most people take. Some claim to be atheists (they "know" there is no God); some profess agnosticism (they don't know whether God exists); and others are "believers" (they believe that some form of higher being does exist). The last group usually believes that there is some purpose in life beyond a physical existence on earth.

Many an alcoholic grew up with a belief in God fostered by his or her parents' attendance at a particular church. As the child matured, he or she may have discovered that some of the religious beliefs learned in Sunday school no longer fit real life needs and experiences. For the alcoholic, this conflict often was a part of the beginning of a drinking pattern. As we continued to drink, we could quite conveniently reject God and declare ourselves atheists.

I have met few alcoholics who are truly atheistic, although many enter treatment or come to AA claiming they are.

The most common type of alcoholic "atheist" has reached an intellectual conclusion about God and religion. This kind of atheist can usually quote humanist philosophers, and typically embraces a human-oriented value system. If this alcoholic is able to use some of the pointers we've discussed so far and can continue to drink, he can go happily on his way with his self-imposed atheism intact.

*   *   *

Many alcoholics consider themselves agnostic. They once believed in God, but their drinking experiences have caused them to question their earlier convictions. They hold on to many of the values they learned as children, but can't make them apply to the world as they've learned it exists. Their solution is not to reject God, but to simply write Him off as irrelevant.

As a teenager, I once heard a fundamentalist minister urge the parents in his congregation not to send their sons and daughters to college. "It's a proven fact," he said, "that more than fifty percent of the young people who leave this community and go to college never return to the church. Their souls are lost."

As one of the souls he considered lost, one reason I never returned to "the church" was that I met black people, Jews, Catholics, Methodists, Moslems and Hindus, all of whom my minister had assigned to the pits of hell, and I simply couldn't reconcile what he had told me about these people with the way they really were. I also had my first encounter with a member of a rival fundamentalist denomination, who insisted that *I* was the one bound for hell because I didn't practice *his* religion.

That's all great stuff for us drinkers. It's an easy step from writing off what misguided ministers have told you to writing off God as an uninvolved factor in life.

* * *

By far the greatest number of alcoholics or heavy drinkers still believe in God, but their need to drink far outweighs their spiritual needs. However, spiritual life is more difficult for the alcoholic who believes in God than it is for the atheist or the agnostic. The believer espouses religious values, and firmly believes that he must live up to these values to be spiritually healthy. But he can't. It is not unusual to meet an alcoholic who attends church regularly, but you might also find this person in the drugstore almost every Saturday, buying mouthwash and breath mints for the Sunday service.

If you want to continue drinking, which spiritual belief will serve your purposes best? Any of them. According to findings by those involved in treatment of alcoholism, you'll resist better if you're an intellectual atheist. You don't have quite so much self-pity to muddle around in, and you can use your intelligence to sidetrack a lot of reformers.

Many of the attitudes that help us resist reform can be brought to play in the fight against those espousing spiritual values. The feeling of isolation, for example, is a primary symptom of spiritual illness. In our spiritual lives, just as in our social lives, we may feel that we don't fit. We may feel that we're somehow different from other people, and (combined effectively with that esoteric mixture of grandiosity and self-pity) we may think we're unique and that nobody—including God—understands. We may feel separate from nearly everybody and everything. We may see life as a matter of us against the world, with God sitting out there on a cloud somewhere keeping a scorecard of our screwups.

If we follow this train of logic, we'll have no trouble continuing our old drinking habits. Amen.

8
Getting Off the Wagon

Lots of people think we're crazy because drinking is so important to us.

It's easy to see why those who don't share our need to drink would shake their heads and murmur, "You'd think he would learn" whenever they encounter a "problem drinker" or an alcoholic who has progressed into the nether regions of the disease.

The connection between drinking and destructive behavior becomes quite clear in many cases, and it does indeed seem insane that these types of alcoholics continue to drink despite the terrible things that happen whenever they uncork a bottle.

But the insanity of alcoholism usually works to our benefit; that is, many of us honestly don't recognize how bizarre our behavior is. I was director of a Peace Corps program in the Micronesian Islands a few years before alcohol replaced altruism as my passion. We were conducting a training program on one of the outer islands, where alcohol was taboo. A representative from Washington, D.C., visited our program and found it difficult to believe that he would have to forego his habitual six o'clock martini. He accepted the news with relative good cheer, but became restless and agitated later in the evening. He commented that it was the first time in nearly a decade that he had gone twenty-four hours without a drink. He cut his visit to our island several days short.

I believe my colleague from Washington was truly

unaware of his drinking problem, because I followed his example with remarkable precision. After leaving Micronesia, I spent several years in Washington, where it is not unusual to drink lunch, attend a before-dinner cocktail party, and talk with friends over after-dinner drinks until the wee hours. It is possible—and likely—for an alcoholic to miss the early warning signs of the disease simply because there has not been enough abstinence to contrast with the drinking.

Incidentally, the reason the citizens of our Micronesian outpost outlawed alcohol was that drunkenness had become a major social problem for them. Unfortunately, the social problem that replaced drunkenness was the sniffing of gasoline in outboard motors.

So, regardless of the type of alcoholic we are, or where we may reside geographically or where we may be on the scale of progressive drinking, we are, in fact, crazy. And many folks don't understand the true nature of our nuttiness—nor do we ourselves.

Our insanity may be summarized as the continuation of drinking even after it's obvious (to ourselves, if to nobody else) that the drinking causes problems for us. "Sane" people would stop drinking, right?

Fortunately, people tend to respond to our most obvious symptoms, and professionals tend to treat the same symptoms. However, the minute one symptom is under control, another will pop up in its place. That's one reason families and friends who try to help us can become as crazy as we are, and set themselves up for all kinds of manipulations that allow us to continue our seemingly blissful trips to the neighborhood liquor store or saloon.

The most common approach to sobriety approved by society at large is to encourage the alcoholic to stop drinking. This makes such good horse sense that you immediately suspect it must be wrong. And it is.

It's like those simple plans folks at the feed store in

my native Ozarks keep coming up with to solve government's problems. They make sense, but government is not a simple, rational organization, so it isn't logical to reform it in a simple, rational way. It isn't rational for an alcoholic to drink, so it's crazy to use rational arguments in urging us to quit. Aversion therapy, in which the alcoholic is encouraged to drink until he or she becomes violently ill, is based somewhat on the idea that what's illogical to an alcoholic becomes logical. But that approach doesn't work very well, either. We're sneaky enough to be logical when it serves our purposes, and we know perfectly well that it wasn't the booze that made us sick, it was the manner in which we were forced to drink it, or it was the pills or shots that were given to us before we drank. Besides, if we're going to drink until we're sick, we want to do it *our* way.

Sometimes it frightens us when somebody starts to zero in on any one area in which we know we are vulnerable. The experienced drinker soon learns, however, there's little to fear. We can close this window of vulnerability quickly, with nobody the wiser. What some of our would-be reformers don't understand is that by shutting down one problem area, they're simply forcing us to retreat into a safer area.

Let's take the worst possible case—the situation most likely to strike terror in our hearts. Suppose we've done something really dramatic, such as wrecking the car, getting arrested, hitting somebody, getting fired, etc. One of the biggies, in other words. An apology won't do it this time. The wife or husband says, "This time I've had it. I'm not coming back until you stop drinking." The bags are packed and the kids have on their coats.

It's time to bite the bullet. You'll probably have to stop drinking.

"Wait a minute," you're probably saying. "What are you suggesting?"

Well, a few periods of abstinence won't hurt you, and I'll guarantee that you'll be drinking again soon. As a matter of fact, you won't be able *not* to be drinking again soon. If you stop drinking but don't do anything else, such as start attending AA meetings, get an AA sponsor, or enter a treatment program, you'll be dry for a time, but your feelings and behavior will be much the same as they were when you were drinking. Veterans call this "white knuckle" sobriety. There's no serenity or comfort, and you'll need a drink desperately most of the time. Your family will observe your suffering and will probably be impressed by your display of will power. They'll probably feel better, even if you don't, and they'll begin to soften.

The first few times you pull the "on the wagon" trick, a couple of weeks will do it. You can proudly announce that you've got the demon brew licked, and you can take it or leave it. The family applauds, and you decide at that point not to leave it any longer, but to take it in massive amounts. Glorious binges frequently follow forced abstinence. This cycle is usually good for a few encores, and if the required abstinence time grows longer with each episode, you can always learn how to sneak a few drinks on the side.

*　　*　　*

There's still one final defense for anyone who wishes to continue drinking.

Even if you were forced into AA or treatment, and you've been sober now for two, six, or even twelve months, you are by no means defeated. So what if you're going to AA and you're beginning to feel somewhat different about yourself?

What's the problem? You're not drinking—that's the problem!

What to do about this unusual state of affairs? Have no fear. It's very easy to return to active drinking. It's so easy, in fact, that lots of folks who have renewed their relationship with the bottle after a time away have done so with little or no conscious effort.

On the other hand, some "relapses" (that's what the do-gooders at AA call it when we start drinking again after having stopped for a while) require a degree of diligence. Drinkers who have enjoyed this type of relapse may tell you they got drunk just in time. They had started to enjoy sobriety, and their lives were coming together. They were spending so much time and energy working on *not* drinking that they actually lost their perspective. Fortunately, they eventually became complacent about not drinking and started taking it for granted. When this happened, their return to drinking was assured.

I once passed up a beautiful relapse opportunity a couple of months after I had completed a treatment program. After a slow-pitch softball game, one of the players from the other team came over, said "Nice game," and tossed me a beer. I had the top popped before I remembered that I was not supposed to drink anymore. I don't know what was wrong with me. I could have had an easy return to drinking and everybody would have known it was purely accidental. Sobriety—even a little of it—can sure screw you up.

Even if relapse doesn't happen of its own accord, a person may pave its way by instigating a policy of "benign neglect" toward sobriety. This approach paves the way for the soon-to-be reactivated alcoholic. He or she doesn't do anything overtly to prevent sobriety, but neither are any positive steps taken to protect sobriety. Alcoholism loves to meet folks who offer no resistance; if they're not working to keep their sobriety, they probably won't be sober long.

*   *   *

Even if you have stopped drinking and have lost contact with your old playmates and playgrounds, and bought into AA's propagandized lifestyle, you may easily regain admission to the drinking world. Here's how.

What could be simpler than to start at the point where sobriety became somewhat stable, and work backwards to the point where drinking is once again in the driver's seat? We know, of course, that different individuals may stop drinking at different points, and by the same token may succeed in relapsing at various points. But this will provide the general idea.

The first step toward successful relapse is to stop going to AA meetings, and aftercare if you've been through a treatment program, stop calling your sponsor (and don't return his or her calls), don't read your *A Day at a Time* message each morning, and don't say the "Serenity Prayer." I've talked to hundreds of alcoholics who experienced relapses, and everyone failed to do at least one of the four things listed above. On the other hand, I don't believe I have ever met a person who relapsed while doing these four things on a daily basis. Another way of looking at it is that it takes a one hundred percent effort to stay sober, but a twenty-five percent effort will allow a rewarding relapse.

There's no excuse for staying sober!

It is also important to our drinking that we remain in touch with other people who are experiencing trouble staying off the sauce. Simply because a person has gained some sobriety, you don't have to cross him or her off your list of drinking pals. This is true regardless of how long the person has been sober, whether he or she has been through one or a dozen treatment programs, or whether the person practically lives at the AA meeting place. People do go back to drinking, and this blessed event may take place at any time for any alcoholic.

The sneaky thing about sobriety is that, no matter how bravely we fight against it, we usually feel good once we have it. Things seem to start going our way, our Higher Power seems to be smiling on us, and we're amazed at how much more reasonable and charming our friends have become. You'd think *they* were the ones who had sobered up. Relapse, logically, should be the furthest thing from a recovering alcoholic's mind.

Thank goodness, logic has little to do with drinking. As a result, a return to drinking for even the most enthusiastic, chest-pounding AA disciple is usually closer to happening than one would think. This isn't as weird as it may sound.

What happens when we feel good? If we feel good, we usually don't feel sick. If we don't feel sick, it follows that we're well. If we're well, we don't have our disease anymore, and if we don't have our disease anymore, guess what? Yep. Down the hatch. Let's face it—peace, serenity and happiness are just too much to handle all at once.

All this may sound confusing, but some expert has come up with a checklist that should help simplify the return to drinking for you. The list was intended to help people identify danger signs so they could prevent relapses. But there's no law saying you can't use it to promote a relapse, or to help urge one on a recovering friend. If you do the following things, or even a few of them, I personally guarantee success:

- Stop going to AA.

- Stop attending aftercare, if you were in a treatment program.

- Stop reading your *A Day at a Time* messages and saying the "Serenity Prayer."

- Start doubting your ability to stay sober.

- Decide that being abstinent is all you need.
- Become overconfident about staying sober.
- Avoid talking about your problems and your sobriety.
- Behave compulsively, overwork or underwork, hog the conversation or withdraw, etc.
- Overreact to stressful situations.
- Start isolating yourself.
- Become preoccupied with one area of your life.
- Do nothing about minor depressions.
- Start unrealistic or haphazard planning.
- Live in the "there and then."
- Worry about your life plan failing.
- Start idle daydreaming and wishful thinking.
- Look at your problems as unsolvable.
- Avoid having fun.
- Overanalyze yourself.
- Become irritated with friends and family.
- Begin blaming people, places, things, and conditions for your problems.
- Begin doubting you ever drank too much.
- Eat irregularly.
- Sleep irregularly.
- Progressively lose your daily routine.
- Develop an "I don't care" attitude.
- Openly reject help.
- Rationalize that drinking or using drugs can't make your life worse than it is now.

- Feel sorry for yourself.
- Have fantasies about social drinking.
- Begin to lie consciously.
- Increase your use of nonprescription medications.
- Completely lose confidence in yourself.
- Develop unreasonable resentments.
- Become overwhelmed with loneliness, frustration, anger and tension.
- Begin visiting old drinking friends and places.
- Convince yourself you never, ever, ever *really* had a drinking problem.
- Start drinking or using a chemical that is not your drug of choice.
- Practice controlled drinking or drug use.

If this list is too long to remember, or if you're having too much fun sober to get around to a relapse, you might find greater success by turning an old AA saying on its head. This saying is one of those trite, cute little things that sober people go around quoting all the time:
If you want to stay sober, don't get too:

H ungry A ngry L onely T ired

*   *   *

There you have it. If you can't fight off sobriety after you've absorbed all this information, you might as well resign yourself to a life without liquor.

Let's review the situation before the contest begins again in earnest.

You know that reformers will hit you with every weapon they have on the disease of alcoholism. They'll tell you that it's no disgrace to suffer from it. They'll point out that the disease is one hundred percent treatable and that you can put it into permanent remission. They'll point out in great detail all the damage it has done to you in every area of your life (as if you didn't know already).

When simple reasoning doesn't work, the reformers will get nasty. They'll start making you take responsibility for your own actions; they'll stop making it easier for you to drink (they won't "enable" you anymore, in their terms) and they'll start getting help for themselves so they can break the hold you seem to have on them. They'll even set traps for you. They'll try to force you into a corner where your only realistic alternative is treatment and/or AA.

They'll tell you about how wonderful life is without drinking: how you can achieve your goals; how you can live happily and comfortably, and maintain an existence of serenity and gratitude. They'll talk about how your friends and family will come back to you.

Occasionally, what they're telling you will sound enticing. But, once again, don't give up. In fact, the odds are overwhelmingly in our favor. We can take advantage of the continuing ignorance about the disease among non-alcoholics, be they relatives or friends or medical doctors or psychiatrists. We can call on the dozens of excuses, rationalizations, and deceptions that are outlined in this book. We can summon our Triple-D's—*Denial, Detour*, and *Delay*—when some crisis threatens our drinking.

We can work to perfect our stinkin' thinkin' even during periods of forced abstinence. We can make certain that our attitudes remain intact. We can make our personalities and our behavior reflect our attitudes so people will eventually leave us in peace with the bottle.

We can turn our backs to spiritual issues by focusing on the shortcomings of humankind, secure in our knowledge that a Higher Power will not appear without our cry for help.

We can bide our time through periods of forced sobriety—and even treatment—knowing that a relapse is at our fingertips at any given moment. Sobriety does not come with a lifetime guarantee.

One last thing: Victory can be yours if you simply realize that no person or place or condition on earth can take your active drinking from you against your will.

You can love the bottle—or you can love life. The decision is yours and yours alone.

9

My Own Story

I suspect the string has run out. It's confession time. It probably will come as no surprise to most of you that I've been telling a series of whopping lies about how to cope with alcoholism and my personal experience with drinking.

The truth is that I had my last drink of alcohol (vodka, mixed with Dr. Pepper—doesn't that sound tasty?) in the early morning hours of June 4, 1980, as I was packing to enter the Edgewood Chemical Dependency Program in St. Louis. I have failed to return to drinking, despite constant relapse opportunities, since that fateful day.

Before you pass judgment on me, let me tell you a little of my story. Perhaps you'll learn something from my experience that you can use to either gain or avoid sobriety, depending on your objective.

I am living proof that AA is correct when it speaks of alcohol as "cunning, baffling, and powerful." There is no rational person on the face of the earth who would look at my personal history and predict that I would ever become a drinker, much less an alcoholic.

I was born and reared on a farm near a little community in southwest Missouri. My parents were, and are, hard-working, caring people whose primary ambition was to provide their four children the best education possible. Neither my father nor my mother ever drank. My two sisters and my brother don't drink. One sister's personal experience with alcohol consists entirely of one-half can of beer she drank while in college. She decided immediately that she wanted no more to do with the foul-tasting stuff. As far as my family and I can determine, I have no blood relatives who abused alcohol. In fact, we're hard-pressed to find anyone in my family tree who drank at all.

This does not mean, of course, that a group of my ancestors did not, a few generations ago, shove an imbibing relative into a closet and deny to the world that he or she had ever existed. There is also the possibility that I'm the first sprout on the alcoholic branch of our tree. We know, however, that it isn't really important at this point to determine why I became alcoholic. The important thing is that I am an alcoholic, and that my children and their children's children realize that they are at risk if they choose to drink or to use other drugs.

Protestant churches abound in my hometown. Within a four-mile radius of the town, which has an official population of 208, there are four denominations: Christian, Methodist, Baptist, and Church of Christ. While there is considerable bickering from the pulpits of these respective sects concerning who is and is not bound for hell because of the building they choose on Sunday mornings, I can't even, in all honesty, blame hellfire-and-brimstone preachers and the nosy and hypocritical morality of neighbors for my drinking. As I mentioned in an earlier chapter, fundamentalist churches and conservative communities make easy targets for alcoholics as they cast about for reasons to drink. The dogmatic rigidity of the churches did indeed cause confusion on my part as I grew up, and I certainly took advantage of them to place blame for my drinking in later years.

But, by and large, the people in my home community are a live-and-let-live bunch, surprisingly liberal for their demographics, supportive of their native children.

Virtually everyone in town knew I drank too much, even though I pretended to myself and to others that I hid it successfully, and most people knew when I went into treatment. I'll never forget the overwhelming warmth and acceptance I received from the entire community when I returned from treatment. I don't know if I could have survived the first few months of sobriety without the love and understanding of the people of Dadeville, Missouri. And one minister, who also is a lifetime teacher, has given me invaluable support in all my efforts.

My parents were about as nonjudgmental as parents can be. They always took us children to one or another of the churches, they required and enforced "good" behavior based on a basic set of principles and values, but they were not dogmatic in dealing with their kids, their neighbors, or anyone else. They never condemned anyone for drinking. They simply didn't drink themselves, and viewed it as a waste of time, money, and talent.

Like many small towns throughout the country, the local school was my community's focus of interest, achievement, and entertainment. High school sports, particularly basketball, dominated everybody's conversation. For many local residents, lifelong reputations were developed on the basketball court when they were teen-agers. It is not unusual, even today, to attend the funeral of an elderly community resident and find the major topic of conversation to be what a fine basketball player the old gent had been as a junior and senior in high school.

Because of this intense interest in sports, not many young people drank when I was in high school. Most of us didn't even smoke cigarettes. We'd have been kicked off the team if the coach so much as heard rumors of our smoking or drinking.

From age five or six, I thought of little besides being

an above-average basketball and baseball player. When I had the good fortune not only to achieve this goal, but to be a good student as well, life looked very promising at seventeen. I, the future alcoholic, graduated from high school having tasted exactly one sip of warm beer in my life—and I hadn't even swallowed that.

My real exposure to drinking came in college. Again, I was much more interested in playing basketball than anything else, so I didn't down my beer or bourbon and Seven-Up with the same enthusiasm as some of my fraternity brothers. In fact, I became so sick the first time I really drank, that it was more than a year before I did more than nurse a beer and pretend to drink more than I actually did. Even when I interrupted my education to spend six months with the Marine Corps Reserve, I did little drinking. I had exactly two beers the evening of my twenty-first birthday.

So there I was, the soon-to-be alcoholic, graduating from college, disliking the taste of booze and the sensation it gave me. I estimate my total intake of alcohol during four years of college and six months in the Marines at about two cases of beer and two fifths of bourbon. About two days' worth, in other words, for later times and later places. So much for several dozen theories about how alcoholics are made, right?

To top if off, I had several fraternity brothers who drank heavily throughout college. One fellow would swallow a six-pack of beer, vomit, and down another within a matter of a minute or two. He used to do that at river parties to entertain the rest of us and our dates. He and most of my classmates who drank substantially in college did not become alcoholics.

I majored in English and physical education in college, intending to be a high school coach and teacher. In fact, shortly before graduation, I signed a teaching contract with my hometown school for the following year.

Although I didn't talk much about it, I really didn't feel ready to settle down in that role. Meanwhile, something happened that changed my life forever.

I used to wonder if I would have become an alcoholic if I hadn't been stirred by President John F. Kennedy's demand: "Ask not what your country can do for you; ask instead what you can do for your country." The answer, of course, is yes. Nevertheless, I later became quite effective at using the three D's and convincing people that President Kennedy and the Peace Corps made me drink so much.

At any rate, when I heard President Kennedy talk about the Peace Corps, I applied, was accepted, broke my teaching contract, and set off to Tunisia with a bunch of people who were as idealistic, and as dissatisfied with life's options at that point, as I was. And, for the first time, I began to enjoy drinking.

Though I didn't want to admit it, I felt insecure among my new colleagues. I had grown up in a tiny community, had attended a small college, and had no idea how to dress or behave around folks from the East and West Coasts, who had graduated from institutions such as Harvard and Yale and Smith and Stanford. To top it off, we early Peace Corps volunteers became celebrities of a sort, as the media tried to present to a curious public exactly what kinds of weird kids would traipse off to Africa instead of working toward down payments on station wagons and duplexes in the suburbs.

In addition to the attention newspaper photographers and reporters lavished on us, we were invited to activities hosted by the American ambassador and by the president of Tunisia. State Department people, French expatriates, and an impressive array of suave, continental people from other countries and cultures extended standing invitations to us. This would-be small-town Ozarks basketball coach was overwhelmed by the sophistication that seemed to engulf our group. I was awed and a bit frightened by this new environment. I also liked it.

It didn't take long for me to learn that whatever discomfort I felt at these social gatherings disappeared after a cocktail or two. I also discovered that I was a better conversationalist than I had thought, and that I had the ability to make friends among a group of people whom I considered to be superior to me in terms of wealth and the social niceties.

Don't get me wrong. The Peace Corps did not consist of an endless cocktail circuit on Embassy Row. The vast bulk of my time was spent as a physical education teacher in a small orphanage near the Algerian border. It was a lonely, rewarding job; it was all the things a stereotypical hairshirt Peace Corps job is supposed to be. Interestingly, I didn't drink while at the work site. I didn't even keep wine or beer on hand. But on the occasions when our group would gather in Tunis, I would look forward to renewing acquaintances and the pleasant feeling a couple of cocktails would provide. I rarely, however, became intoxicated.

Near the end of my two years in Tunisia, I signed another coaching contract with my hometown high school. The problem was that when I returned, nothing there seemed to have changed, while it seemed that I had changed a great deal. With snatches of Thomas Wolfe's *You Can't Go Home Again* (Wolfe, incidentally, was also a prodigious boozer) running through my head, I once again broke my contract. I boarded a plane in Springfield, Missouri, landed in Washington, D.C., walked off the street into Peace Corps headquarters, asked for a job, and was hired. *Everybody* who worked in Washington at that time had drinks for lunch, drinks after work, and drinks before and after dinner. I needed to be a part of the group, didn't I?

Things moved quickly and successfully. I met an intelligent, attractive young woman while on a recruiting trip for the Peace Corps. We were married a few months later, and I moved up the bureaucratic and creative ranks of the Peace Corps from staff writer to director of radio and television to executive secretary of the agency. Drinking was an everyday ritual by now, but I rarely overdid it. I usually didn't even keep booze at home.

My wife, Suzie, wanted to fulfill her dream of going overseas with the Peace Corps, so I accepted a position as Director of the Mariana Island Peace Corps program in Micronesia. Since I was one of the youngest overseas directors at that time, my ambitions soared. Ambassador to an important country, I decided, was the least I should expect from my talents. Certainly, I could be a member of Congress, and maybe, well, I had, after all, developed a few Kennedy-esque affections. Who knows?

Micronesia is an island nation in the middle western Pacific which was, at that time, administered by the U.S. Department of the Interior through a United Nations mandate. Our country had done an embarrassingly inept job of running Micronesia, which we Peace Corps people were quick to point out to the resident Interior Department types. My days in Micronesia were filled with conflict, screaming and shouting, beautiful Pacific island scenery, and an incredible amount of drinking. My drinking habits, and those of many others in Micronesia, increased. I always drank at noon and at night, and sometimes in the mornings.

The Vietnam War intruded upon our lives in Micronesia, as it did for practically all Americans. Needing additional air bases in the Pacific, the U.S. Department of Defense decided to claim some Micronesian lands under an old eminent domain clause, with no compensation for the native landowners. We in the Peace Corps objected, some of our volunteer lawyers began representing Micronesian citizens in court against the U.S., and I, along with my fellow dissenters, was ordered back to the U.S.

You can imagine, I'm sure, how detrimental this was to my career, and what a break it was for my burgeoning case of alcoholism. How many alcoholics do you know who can blame Richard Nixon, Henry Kissinger, and William Westmoreland for their drinking problem? People were altogether too willing to nod sympathetically and pour me another drink when I would explain how Nixon had prevented me from being appointed ambassador to some exotic land.

Suzie and I returned to Washington, D.C., and renewed old friendships. I found a terrific job with a private social action firm which was established and administered primarily by former Peace Corps people. I was welcomed warmly as somewhat of a hero, having confronted the evil Nixon empire.

Things should have been wonderful. In late summer, 1970, Suzie flew back to Micronesia and brought four-month-old David, our newly adopted son, back home with her. I was involved in politics and writing, and filled with self-importance. I was also drinking at least a fifth of booze daily—good stuff, like Beefeaters Gin and Johnny Walker Black. Only places that took credit cards were good enough for lunch and for after-work cocktails.

But something was different. Even among heavy drinkers, my drinking was different. I was drinking more than my friends and I wasn't stopping when they did. I was beginning to become belligerent just when they were beginning to have a good time. I began complaining about all the injustices done to me. Coworkers started finding excuses not to have lunch with me. I started drinking alone more and more and discovered that I liked it. I always kept booze at home.

My company opened an office in San Francisco. Suzie was delighted, and largely through her efforts, I was sent out to help run the new operation. Suzie and David went out ahead of me, and by the time I arrived, we owned a house in Mill Valley that had once belonged to Mama Cass.

I honestly remember very little about that year in San Franscisco. I remember driving my Austin-Healey from Mill Valley through a rainbow tunnel across the Golden Gate into San Francisco every day. I remember wearing a three-piece suit to work, along with a headband around my shoulder-length hair. I remember not having enough work to keep me busy and spending nearly all day, most days, in respectable bars around town, and driving back to Mill Valley at night. I remember resenting flower children bringing their sleeping bags into my house for days at a time, eating all my food and stinking up the place with marijuana while they criticized me for drinking establishment booze. I remember flying off on business trips all the time, and of feeling guilty once in a while about neglecting David. I remember the meeting Suzie and I had with a divorce lawyer. I remember driving my Austin-Healey back to Washington, D.C., from San Francisco. And I remember Suzie sending David back to me for good because she said she couldn't care for him.

Before David arrived to live with me, I had quit my job and was subsisting on unemployment checks and consulting jobs around Washington. I liked the consulting jobs, which consisted primarily of writing business proposals and reports for government agencies and consulting firms. Anyone can make a decent living in Washington if he or she can put simple sentences together. I'm convinced that nobody in the federal government has ever taken a high school English class. More importantly, I could do most of the work at home and was free to drink as I worked.

I began to pull myself together a bit when David came. I rented a townhouse, found a good baby-sitter, and took a full-time job as, of all things, a drug abuse counselor at the National Drug Abuse Training Center—the showpiece of President Nixon's ballyhooed war on drugs. I would have a morning drink, go to work, plan programs for heroin and cocaine addicts ("real" drug abusers, in other words), have three, four, or five martinis for lunch, go back and deal with drug problems for a few more hours, then home to David and an evening of drinking.

Shortly after this new cycle began, I met Emmy, my present wife, whose sister had married my best friend from the Peace Corps in Tunisia. Emmy invited David and me to her place for a barbeque one Sunday, and nine days later we were married.

Emmy, fortunately, was a teacher, so my financial situation, which had become quite strained, was eased a bit. This allowed me to quit my job and work on what had become my obvious destiny—author of the *really* great American novel. The only problem was that nobody seemed to appreciate my talent. No matter how much I wrote, or how loudly I told of my abilities and the important people I knew and how Richard Nixon had it in for me, it didn't seem to do any good.

I stayed home and drank more and more often. I had, however, switched from liquor to wine. I had convinced Emmy that wine wasn't as bad for me as hard liquor. Besides, I couldn't afford good booze any longer. Emmy, thankfully, was turning into a fine enabler and usually offered me the solace I needed as the cold, cruel world closed in on me. Emmy understood why I needed to drink, and she never seemed to grow tired of endless hours of conversation in which I would come incredibly close to discovering the secrets of the universe.

Finally, in early 1976, it became quite clear to me that I didn't have a real drinking problem. Emmy, David and I had a geographical problem. Anybody, in those post-Watergate days, would drink a lot if they had to stay in Washington. A relocation seemed the ideal solution to all our problems.

Emmy and I both signed teaching contracts at—you guessed it—my old hometown school. We loaded our belongings into a rented truck and moved from Washington to Missouri. As part of the deal, I had promised Emmy I would stop drinking cold turkey. Well, I almost did. I carried only one bottle under the seat in the truck and took a nip from it only when I really felt the need.

My drinking increased once we were back in my old community, even though I enjoyed teaching and coaching. I thought nobody suspected that I was drinking most mornings before I went to school and every evening after school. Sometimes I would rush home and have a drink at lunchtime or during my free period, and sometimes I would carry a bottle to school with me in my briefcase.

Finances began to be a real problem, since teachers don't make much money, especially in small, rural schools. Emmy was also feeling more and more stress, particularly when she couldn't find anybody who would believe her when she told them I drank too much.

It became quite clear to me that Emmy was my problem, especially after she discovered Al-Anon. After three years of arguing about my drinking, she suddenly stopped bugging me and laid down a few rules. There was obviously only one thing to do: I filed for divorce.

Divorce didn't solve as many problems as I thought it would. I wasn't reaching my goals any better than when I was married. I had thought that I wouldn't drink quite so much with Emmy not around to force me to the bottle. That turned out not to be the case. I began drinking even more. Having David half the time (the divorce judge had awarded Emmy and me joint custody) gave me a feeling of fulfillment, but there was a terrible vacuum when he was gone. I would see Emmy once in a while and feel myself weakening. The thought that I needed to stop drinking kept running through my head.

Finally, I couldn't fight it anymore. Even my parents, who had originally joined me in blaming Emmy for my drinking, now told me I had to do something about my alcoholism. I called Emmy and told her I would enter a treatment program if she would make the arrangements. I bought two last fifths of vodka and began to pack.

Once I was actually admitted into the treatment program and started feeling a little better, it didn't take me long to decide that I had been manipulated. It was clear that I had been forced into a treatment program by a family that simply didn't understand the insurmountable problems I was facing. I decided to make the best of a bad situation anyway. I discovered that one patient had completed the program in twenty-one days. So priding myself on my intelligence and girding myself with grandiosity, I decided I could finish in no more than twenty days. Having not been intimately acquainted with many alcoholics (I wasn't unusual in the fact that I hated to be around drunks), I considered myself the best con man around. After all, I had fooled everybody except my immediate family for years. My plan was to float through the program and do what everybody thought should be done, leave after twenty days and be well. I did make one concession to alcoholism. I resolved that I would drink only socially once I had completed the program.

Everything went reasonably well for the first ten days or so. Reading the material and spouting it back was no problem. I had always been a good student, with a good memory. It was also helpful that I had already acquired a lot of information about alcoholism. Emmy had been bringing AA and Al-Anon literature home for years and leaving it lying around as a subtle reminder that I might benefit from it. I had absorbed all that material for a good and logical purpose; I took everything out of context and used it against my wife. This approach is a bit like reading the Bible solely to prove or disprove a point.

The only trouble the counselors gave me in the early days came as a result of my insistence that I wasn't really an alcoholic. I hadn't lost any jobs, I'd never been arrested, etc., etc. I also kept talking about going home after a week and a half, since I had learned everything the program had to offer. I was, in fact, getting a little thirsty. But I just needed one drink. One, as everybody knows, doesn't hurt anything.

Finally, to please them and get them off my back, I said, "Okay, I'm an alcoholic. Now can we get on with it?"

It wasn't that simple. AA has a First Step that says, "We admitted we were powerless over alcohol; that our lives had become unmanageable." The counselors wanted me to memorize that line and repeat it every time I talked to them. It should have been a snap, but for some reason I couldn't recite the thing out exactly the way it was written. I decided it was because it was written in such a heavy-handed way.

At any rate, I stumbled through the first twenty days with no sign that I was making any progress. People who had been new to the program when I arrived kept getting assignments to do their Fourth Step inventories, a sure sign that their departure dates were approaching quickly. No talk about the Fourth Step for me.

"Have you taken the First Step, Jerry?"

"Of course, I have. I took it a couple of weeks ago. You just won't believe me."

"Let's hear you say it."

"Sure, 'We admitted we were powerless over alcohol; that we couldn't manage our lives'."

"It's 'that our lives had become unmanageable,' Jerry. Keep working on it."

I thought about leaving, but didn't because I didn't want to disappoint my parents, my ex-wife and my son.

Treatment had also become a real challenge. Both of my counselors were recovering addicts, and they knew exactly which rocks to turn over to discover where I had hidden my secrets. One of the counselors was about 6'3" and weighed about 240 pounds so I couldn't even intimidate anybody physically.

On the twenty-eighth day, I finally lost my cool. "If you know so damned much about the First Step, why the hell don't you tell me how to take it?" I asked.

The counselor leaned back and smiled. "That's the first positive thing you've done since you got here," he said.

"What? Get angry?"

"No, you asked for help. You don't ask for help very often, do you?"

"I don't need help very often," I said.

"Will you admit that you need help with the First Step?"

"Okay. I need help with the First Step. How do I take it?"

"I can't tell you," the counselor said. He was smirking. I told him I didn't think professional people were supposed to smirk, but it didn't faze him.

"You know," I said, "I'm really tired of playing your mind games. You tell me I need help to take the First Step but you won't help me."

"I just did," the counselor said.

"So what am I supposed to do?"

"You figure it out. I thought you considered yourself pretty smart."

I started for the door after saying something thoroughly unspiritual. "Jerry?" the counselor called. I turned. "Talk to your Higher Power."

It took a couple more days of frustration before I fi-

I once overheard a couple of counselors discussing their patients' apparent need for a visible spiritual awakening. Mostly in jest—but not totally—they considered the merits of wiring up one of their patient rooms with lights and sound. Whenever they encountered a patient whose progress was lagging as he or she awaited a sign from on high, they would assign the patient to that room. In the middle of the night, lights would flash and a Bill Cosby-like voice would boom out: "Barney! This is God, Barney. Get sober or else, Barney!"

Once spirituality begins to creep up on you, your outlook on life will begin to change. You'll start to notice things you haven't seen, sometimes for years. You'll find yourself with a new attitude toward yourself and toward other people. You'll start doing things like letting others finish what they're saying before you interrupt, actually hearing what they're saying, and discovering that some people you had written off are pretty bright after all.

You'll find people listening to what you have to say, but you won't be talking so often or so vehemently. Little things won't bug you so much. You'll allow other people to make mistakes, and you'll take responsibility for your own mistakes. You'll find that most problems have solutions, but none of the solutions involve the use of alcohol.

When these things start to happen to you; when you start to enjoy other people and the things around you; when you start looking forward to new days and to new experiences; when you start to hum or whistle for no apparent reason whatsoever; when some little frustration pops up and you find yourself murmuring, "God grant me the serenity to accept the things I cannot change, the courage to change the things I can, and the wisdom to know the difference"; when these kinds of things start happening to you, you may not stay sober for the rest of your life, but I'll guarantee you one thing: your drinking will be ruined for as long as you live.

One more thing about religion. No matter how devout people are, religion does not protect them from alcoholism. Conversely, as we have seen, there are things about some religions that can actually aid and abet alcoholism.

Alcoholism is present in every religion. Interestingly enough, it is more prevalent in those religions which condone the use of alcohol in a social sense, and in those religions that condemn its use in any sense.

I had the pleasure of spending some time with a delightful alcoholic a few years ago. He was a Catholic priest who had been ordered into a treatment program by his superiors. In most respects, this man had the gentle and insightful demeanor one would expect of a priest, but when it came to his own alcoholism, he acted and reacted just like any of the rest of us. He used *Denial, Delay* and *Detour* like a master, and he held considerable unpriestly resentments against those he considered responsible for depositing him in the midst of a bunch of drunks.

He also had a refreshing sense of humor. His flock, it seems, avoided this priest's early masses, but by the last mass of the day it would be standing room only.

"We're supposed to celebrate mass with the fruit of the vine," the priest would say, "and reflect how it represents God's bounty. Is it my fault that my gratitude for God's goodness ran over on occasion? And nowhere," he would usually pound a fist for emphasis at this point, "in any of our instructions does it say how big the chalice should be nor how full one was expected to fill it!" The last mass must have been quite a performance.

The priest's resentment centered upon the event that led to his immediate enrollment in treatment. All that had happened, according to him, is that he was returning from a quiet dinner at which a few cocktails had been served. He was tired, it was a cold and rainy night, and his car slid off the road and into a ditch. It could have happened to anybody. He hadn't been drinking too much. He refused to take the breathalyzer test simply as a matter of principle. He was a priest, after all, and deserved some respect from the police.

About the third week into treatment, the priest sheepishly added a few details to his story. The quiet dinner had started at 2:00 P.M. and had lasted until nearly midnight. The cocktails had consisted of four fifths of whiskey for five priests ("show me four Catholics and I'll show you a fifth," is a favorite line of Father Joseph Martin, a nationally known speaker on alcoholism). The ditch the priest's car had "slid into" was in reality a forty-foot ravine on the other side of an eight-lane expressway. And the priest's blood-alcohol level, when he arrived at the hospital, was .20, highly intoxicated.

A fitting conclusion to this story, I suppose, is that spiritual health is essential to long-term, comfortable sobriety. There are steps the committed alcoholic can take to prevent a spiritual awakening from occurring, but you have to be on your guard against it at all times. It can happen to anybody—even to a priest.

*   *   *

Now that I've come clean with you, I feel better. The fact of the matter is, I like sobriety. I work hard every day to protect my sobriety. My family understands that even they are second in importance to me. Without sobriety, I would have nothing. I would be nothing.

I'm tempted at this point to write, "And they all lived happily ever after, and you can too if you'll stop drinking," but there are a couple of loose ends that should be tied up.

First, as I'm sure you've surmised, Emmy and I were remarried following my treatment. An added feature to this reunion is Melissa, who was born almost exactly nine months following our remarriage. Sobriety does remarkable things. We had tried to have children, without success, throughout my drinking years.

Little successes that seemed so elusive while I was drinking occur almost without effort as I work my program of sobriety. I am moving rapidly toward the academic and professional goal I had set for myself so long ago and then abandoned, and my writing career is blossoming. My family is happy and united, and new gifts and rewards appear almost daily.

When people ask me how they can achieve sobriety, or how they can help someone else give up alcoholic drinking, there is only a simple message I can deliver.

First, do what the folks at AA and at good treatment programs tell you to do. Don't accept short cuts. Work at every step of AA's program. Talk with recovering people and ask for their help. In my opinion, if a person truly wants sobriety, he or she has a good chance of achieving and maintaining it by doing four things daily: 1) Read the *A Day at a Time* book; 2) Say the "Serenity Prayer"; 3) Talk with your sponsor; 4) Go to an AA or NA meeting.

Sobriety is a reachable goal for anybody. There are too many tens of thousands of happy, recovering alcoholics for anyone to argue otherwise.

One more thing. If you are to have sobriety, you have to want it. You must want it more than anything else in the world. You must cherish and protect it. And you must thank your Higher Power every waking moment for helping you attain it.

If you spend much time around recovering alcoholics, you will learn the benefits of sobriety. You will find that recovering people's lives are in order, or gaining order. Their personal and career goals are becoming clearer and more reachable. When they take a stand on an issue, they will do so with the courage of their convictions, not with the bitterness and self-pity they gleaned from a bottle, and for which they'll try to apologize tomorrow.

For me, the greatest reward of sobriety is no longer needing to tell the worst of all lies—the lie that requires you to look into your ten-year-old son's eyes and say that your drinking is hurting no one except yourself.

Appendix A
Are You an Alcoholic?

You've probably done countless little exercises like this, mostly to prove to your husband or wife that you're not an alcoholic. These self-tests show up periodically in *Reader's Digest* and other family magazines, so you've probably come to take them for granted. Be careful with this one, though! It was developed by the folks at Johns Hopkins University, and those people know a thing or two about alcoholism.

To show you how sneaky they are, they don't tell you until after the last question what your score will mean.

Let's see how you fare on this test. Ask yourself each question, and then answer honestly yes or no.

1. Do you lose time from work due to drinking?

2. Is drinking making your home life unhappy?

3. Do you drink because you are shy with other people?

4. Is drinking affecting your reputation?

5. Have you ever felt remorse after drinking?

6. Have you gotten into financial difficulties as a result of drinking?

7. Do you turn to lower companions and an inferior environment when drinking?

8. Does your drinking make you careless of your family's welfare?

9. Has your ambition decreased since drinking?

10. Do you crave a drink at a definite time daily?

11. Do you want a drink the next morning?

12. Does drinking cause you to have difficulty in sleeping?

13. Has your efficiency decreased since drinking?

14. Is drinking jeopardizing your job or business?

15. Do you drink to escape from worries or troubles?

16. Do you drink alone?

17. Have you ever had a complete loss of memory as a result of drinking?

18. Has your physician ever treated you for drinking?

19. Do you drink to build up your self-confidence?

20. Have you ever been to a hospital or institution on account of drinking?

Finished? Okay, here's the kicker. If you answered yes to any one of the questions, there is a definite chance that you may be alcoholic.

If you answered yes to any two, the chances are that you are an alcoholic.

If you have answered yes to three or more, you're definitely an alcoholic.

If the scoring standard seems pretty drastic, it is. Unfortunately, I can vouch for the fact that this test is surprisingly accurate. The only people I've ever evaluated for treatment who passed this test admitted later that they had lied.

The most unbelievable thing about this test, when you stop and think about it, is that most people go through their entire lives without ever doing even one of the items listed.

You'll probably want to keep your test score to yourself. Whatever you do, don't let your husband or wife see your real answers.

Questions reprinted with permission of Comprehensive Care Corporation and Johns Hopkins University.

Appendix B
Understanding Alcoholism

Here's another test. This one is a bit more challenging. The answers follow the test, but it will be more interesting if you don't peek. I know how senseless it is to give that kind of warning to alcoholics, but maybe you could look at it this way. Don't peek the first time. Then take the test again in the presence of your husband or wife and pretend that you've never seen the thing before.

Circle the T for true and the F for false. If you don't know or aren't certain, guess. You only live once, you know.

1. **T F** Most acceptable definitions of alcoholism include reference to the approximate quantity of alcohol consumed per unit of time.

2. **T F** As well as suffering adverse consequences from his drinking, the alcoholic usually drinks according to different patterns than does the normal drinker.

3. **T F** Most health professionals consider alcoholism our number one health problem.

4. **T F** Alcoholism affects approximately one percent of our adult population.

5. **T F** Alcoholism should be considered a symptom of an underlying personality or mental disorder.

6. **T F** Approximately twenty-five percent of all alcoholics are on skid row.

7. **T F** Research has failed to establish any specific genetic, environmental, social, or personality factors as the cause of alcoholism.

8. **T F** Becoming unconscious or passing out from excessive drinking is known as an alcoholic blackout period.

9. **T F** A person who never consumes anything stronger than beer is probably not an alcoholic.

10. **T F** A brief drinking history should be obtained by the doctor from every new patient.

11. **T F** One may be a thoroughly reliable worker on the job and still be alcoholic.

12. **T F** The ability to confine drinking to weekends suggests that a person is probably not alcoholic.

13. **T F** An alcoholic must hit bottom before he can begin the recovery process.

14. **T F** Alcoholics are prone to abuse any other chemical substance given them which also produces a sedative effect.

15. **T F** It is usually wise to conceal liquor when entertaining a recovering alcoholic in your home and to advise relatives of alcoholic persons to do the same.

16. **T F** The suicide rate among alcoholics is markedly higher than that for the general population.

17. **T F** A person's real character emerges when under the influence of alcohol.

18. **T F** Many people who say alcoholism is an illness often behave towards the alcoholic as though he had a moral weakness.

19. **T F** Tranquilizing drugs, such as Librium or Valium, are often valuable in maintaining the recovering alcoholic through his first year or so of sobriety.

20. **T F** An alcoholic with more than ten years of sobriety may safely take an occasional social drink.

21. **T F** Coming from a family background of teetotalism is relative assurance that one will not develop alcoholism.

22. **T F** The first step in psychotherapy with an alcoholic person is determining the underlying reasons for drinking.

23. **T F** Alcoholics Anonymous has been more effective than psychiatric treatment in helping alcoholics recover.

24. **T F** The spouse of the alcoholic is often a primary cause of the alcoholism.

25. **T F** An alcoholic who has "fallen off the wagon" (relapsed into drinking) more than four times may usually be regarded as untreatable.

26. **T F** The strong resistance among alcoholics to admitting their problem is in large part due to society's attitude toward alcoholism.

27. **T F** Involuntary treatment of an unmotivated alcoholic has been shown to be effective in many cases.

28. **T F** Professionals are often wise to advise the spouse of an alcoholic to consider precipitating a crisis, often by separation from the unmotivated alcoholic, after lesser measures have failed.

29. **T F** Many wives of alcoholics tend to become more emotionally disturbed when their husbands are maintaining sobriety.

30. **T F** A spouse or other informant should be interviewed if possible whenever a drinking problem is suspected.

31. **T F** Al-Anon is the companion group to Alcoholics Anonymous for female alcoholics.

32. **T F** Alcoholics often seek help for emotional or family problems without ever mentioning a drinking problem to the interviewer.

33. **T F** Education about alcoholism often helps the alcoholic reduce his resistance to accepting the facts about his condition.

34. **T F** The alcoholic who is maintaining sobriety has no greater number of serious emotional problems than the population in general.

35. **T F** The physician can best help the alcoholic by adding his pleas to that of the family in urging the alcoholic to quit drinking.

36. **T F** Alcoholism can be seen as a type of drug addiction.

37. **T F** A significant emotional problem or disorder generally precedes the development of alcoholism.

38. **T F** Physicians frequently misdiagnose psychiatric problems in alcoholic patients.

39. **T F** The incidence of alcoholism and drug dependence is lower among physicians than among the general population.

Reprinted with permission of Comprehensive Care Corporation.

Answers to Understanding Alcoholism Quiz

1. **False.** Neither the amount of alcohol consumed nor the frequency of drinking determines alcoholism. If one can of beer every six months results in a serious problem —and the person continues to drink that amount at that interval—then alcohol is a problem.

2. **True.** Patterns may vary from one alcoholic to another, and range from periodic binges to heavy daily intake, but the alcoholic drinks in a compulsive manner that sets him apart from the average social drinker.

3. **False.** Even though the World Health Organization ranks alcoholism as the number two health problem worldwide, a surprising number of health professionals remain unaware of the incidence of the disease.

4. **False.** The rate of alcoholism among adults is estimated from a low of ten percent to a high of twenty to twenty-five percent. Nearly seventy-five percent of the population suffers in some way from alcoholism, either as a problem drinker or as a family member or close friend of an alcoholic.

5. **False.** Although alcoholics are frequently diagnosed and treated as mentally disturbed or personality-disordered, less than five percent of all alcoholics have personality problems requiring further treatment once the alcoholic behavior is removed.

6. **False.** According to most estimates, ninety-seven percent of all alcoholics are functioning members of society.

7. **True.** Although it is clear that all these factors contribute to alcoholism, no single, specific cause has been isolated.

8. **False.** An alcoholic blackout is a memory lapse during which the person continues to function, but has little or no recall of what happened during that time.

9. **False.** A can of beer contains about the same amount of alcohol as a shot of whiskey. Beer drinkers tend to consume whatever amount is required to meet their bodies' demand for alcohol.

10. **True.** This applies not only to alcohol treatment facilities. Medical doctors, psychologists and psychiatrists should also obtain this history, since many physical and emotional symptoms may in fact be caused by the primary disease of alcoholism.

11. **True.** Many, if not most, alcoholics are able to function on the job despite their illnesses. Alcoholic men are especially concerned about keeping their jobs, since loss of income would threaten their ability to obtain alcohol. Holding a job also allows the person to deny his problem: "I can't be an alcoholic because I still have a job."

12. **False.** Weekend drinking is not an uncommon alcoholic pattern. The real test is whether the weekend drinking interferes with "normal" family and social life. Are weekends reserved exclusively for drinking activities?

13. **False.** Chemical dependency programs experience about the same rate of successful recovery among those forced into treatment against their will as among those who have lost enough to alcoholism to admit their powerlessness and seek help. Some call this "raising the bottom."

14. **True.** All mood-altering chemicals produce a carry-over effect and cross-tolerance. Denied his drug of choice, the dependent person may maintain his dependency through a different substance. The basic addiction remains, however, and the person usually becomes dependent on all substances which he uses for their mood-altering qualities.

15. **False.** There may be some disagreement on this point, but alcoholics must face the reality that they will not be able to live in an alcohol-free environment.

16. **False.** The suicide rate among alcoholics is about the same as that of the general population.

17. **False.** Quite the contrary. A person's real character is distorted by alcohol. Sobriety brings a return of the true personality.

18. **True.** Although there is a growing awareness that alcoholism is a true disease, many people still have an instinctive attitude toward alcoholics that involves a moral judgment. Even medical professionals may sometimes say the equivalent of: "Yes, alcoholism is a disease; why don't you stop drinking?" This is like asking a heart attack patient to stop having chest pains. The disease, in both cases, needs treatment.

19. **False.** Reputable treatment programs use such drugs for only a very short period—usually from three to five days—while the alcoholic is being detoxified. Long-term maintenance simply prolongs the addiction.

20. **False.** An alcoholic may *never* safely use mood-altering chemicals. Even individuals with twenty or twenty-five years of sobriety suffer relapses when they attempt to drink or use drugs "socially."

21. **False.** If there is alcoholism in the immediate family, the chances of an individual becoming alcoholic are four times greater than if the family is nonalcoholic. However, there is no way to know if a hereditary predisposition to alcoholism is present if alcohol is not used.

22. **False.** The reason a person is alcoholic is because he drinks alcohol. The first step in any therapy should be to eliminate the alcohol.

23. **True.** Psychiatric treatment alone, without the supportive therapy and program offered by AA, has been notoriously unsuccessful in treating alcoholics.

24. **False.** The spouse is frequently targeted for blame by the alcoholic, but no single person has the power to make someone become alcoholic.

25. **False**. Anybody, regardless of how often he or she has failed, may gain sobriety if the recovery program is followed with diligence and total honesty.

26. **True**. Alcoholics themselves frequently have trouble actually believing they have a disease rather than a moral weakness.

27. **True**. The alcoholic may be unmotivated in the beginning, but that attitude can be changed during the course of treatment.

28. **True**. This is called "intervention." However, it is a serious step, and should be taken only with the assistance of trained counselors and therapists. The spouse must also be prepared for the possibility that intervention may fail.

29. **True**. Strangely enough, sobriety may cause serious problems for the nonalcoholic spouse. The nondrinking wife may have assumed some of her husband's roles, and may resist allowing him to resume his place in the family. The wife may also have anger and resentments she can no longer blame on her husband's alcoholism. She may also become jealous of her husband's newfound independence, and of his reliance on AA rather than on her.

30. **True**. Denial is a common defense of alcoholics; they will even use it subconsciously. Information provided by a spouse, other family members or close friends can help considerably in making an accurate assessment.

31. **False**. Al-Anon is the companion group to AA for alcoholic or nonalcoholic relatives and friends of the alcoholic. It includes both men and women. Though most Al-Anon members are nonalcoholic, some are alcoholic themselves, but also have alcoholic friends and family members. These people frequently attend both AA and Al-Anon.

32. **True**. Alcoholics typically want help for the life problems and physical ailments they're experiencing, but they don't want to quit drinking. Therefore, they'll try to focus on the problems rather than on the alcohol. They are more likely to seek help from sources not equipped to deal with alcoholism rather than from professionals in the field of chemical dependency.

33. **True**. Even though the alcoholic typically resists education about the disease, nonjudgmental information does lessen the individual's fear of his condition and makes acceptance of the disease more palatable.

34. **True**. The recovering alcoholic who continues to work his program may in fact experience fewer problems, since he is making a conscious effort to identify and correct the real sources of the problems as they arise.

35. **False**. The physician can best help the alcoholic by honestly stating the nature and extent of the disease and by insisting that the person get specific help to stop drinking. Nor should the physician be an enabler by prescribing medication to ease pain that is directly symptomatic of alcoholism, if such a prescription would delay the alcoholic from receiving treatment.

36. **True**. Alcohol is a major drug, and alcoholism is a major addiction. There is, in fact, persuasive evidence that alcohol is the most dangerous drug in our society.

37. **False**. Although the intake of alcohol and alcoholic behavior may increase after a crisis, alcoholism may develop regardless of the presence or absence of emotional disorders. Most emotionally-disordered people, in fact, are not alcoholics. It is more likely that drinking precedes the emotional problem.

38. **True**. Many of the symptoms of alcoholism resemble psychiatric disorders, particularly thought processes and behaviors. Misdiagnoses are not uncommon.

39. **False**. The incidence is about double that of the general population.

Report Card

"A"   36-39 answers correct. Expert. You're either an alcoholism counselor, a recovering alcoholic, an Al-Anon member, or an alcoholic who has become highly skilled at defending against recovery.

"B"   32-35 answers correct. You have a good general idea about the nature of alcoholism. You probably accept it as a disease, and could be helpful in assisting alcoholics deciding to get help. If you're an alcoholic, you've probably been able to delay treatment for a long time.

"C"   28-31 answers correct. With a little study, you could be in the "B" group. However, you probably need to get rid of some misconceptions about the disease. If you're an alcoholic, you'll be forced into treatment soon; your defenses aren't sophisticated enough.

"D"   24-27 answers correct. Whatever you do, stay away from alcoholics.

"F"   0-23 answers correct. Don't touch an alcoholic with a ten-foot pole. If you're an alcoholic, you probably have no idea what this is all about. You're not interested yet.

Appendix C
The Statistics on Alcoholism

Following are just a few of the consequences of alcoholism in the United States:

—Two out of three murders, one out of three rapes, one out of three suicides, two out of five assaults, and three out of five cases of child abuse are connected to the use of alcohol.

—One out of two deaths by fire and nearly one out of two deaths by drowning are alcohol-related, as are two out of five home accidents.

—One out of two traffic fatalities is alcohol-related in this country every year; twenty-five thousand Americans die in these crashes.

—Driving and drinking results in eight hundred thousand automobile accidents each year.

—One out of every two patients in city hospitals is there because of an alcohol-related problem.

—Diseases involving alcoholism are the third leading cause of premature death in the U.S. Even this stunning figure is misleading, considering the number of alcoholic deaths that are attributed instead to heart disease, cancer, hepatitis, liver and kidney disease, diabetes, suicide, automobile accidents and others.

—Eight thousand young people die in automobile crashes caused by alcohol every year. This is the leading cause of death among young people.

—Forty thousand young adults are disfigured by alcohol-related auto crashes every year.

—National surveys show that one out of three high school students gets drunk at least once a month and three out of five drink once a month or more. One out of five male teenagers and one out of ten female teenagers admit that they sometimes drink until they pass out.

—More than ninety percent of high school seniors have used alcohol.

—Nearly seventy-six percent of high school seniors used alcohol in the month prior to a recent national study.

—Fifty percent of high school seniors drink in cars.

—One of three high school seniors got drunk four or more times in the past year.

—One of seven seniors was drunk at least once each week.

—One of eleven males and one of twenty-five females drink every day.

—Fifty percent of high school seniors had their first experience with alcohol in junior high school.

—One in five teenagers has a problem with alcohol (a "problem" means getting drunk four or more times a year and/or having two or more incidents with the police, a school official, or family members because of drinking).

Reprinted with permission of Life Skills Education, Inc., (1985).

Appendix D
Personalized Disease Chart

Want to have some fun? Find yourself on the following scale of alcoholic progression:

Early Stage

—Sneaks drinks/drugs

—Preoccupied with alcohol/drugs

—Gulps drinks/drugs

—Avoids reference to alcohol/drug use

—Has memory blackouts

—Has increased alcohol/drug tolerance

—Drinks/uses before and after social occasions

—Begins relief drinking/using

—Is uncomfortable in situations without alcohol/ drugs

Middle Stage

—Experiences loss of control

—Is dishonest about alcohol/drug use

—Has increased frequency of relief drinking/using

—Hides and protects supply

—Experiences urgent need for first drink/drug

—Tries periods of forced abstinence

—Others disapprove of drinking/drug use

—Rationalizes drinking/drug usage

—Experiences flashes of aggressiveness

—Exhibits grandiose behavior

—Has guilt about drinking/drug usage

—Neglects eating

—Builds unreasonable resentments

—Devalues personal relationships

—Considers geographic escapes

—Sexual drive decreases

—Quits or loses jobs

—Exhibits unreasonable jealousy

—Drinks/uses alone, secretly

—Tries to control drinking/drug use

Late Stage

—Experiences tremors and shakes

—Experiences early morning drinking/drug use

—Lengthy drinking/drug binges occur

—Thinking is impaired

—Drinks/uses with inferiors

—Loses tolerance for alcohol/drugs

—Has indefinable fears

—Unable to work

—Physical health deteriorates

—Moral standards deteriorate

—Admitted to hospitals/sanitarium

—Feels persistent remorse

—Loses family and friends

—Exhausts all alibis

Final Stage

—Death, jail or insanity

Reprinted with permission of Comprehensive Care Corporation.

Appendix E
Where to Go for Help

There is no need for anyone who is experiencing problems with alcohol, whether personally or as a "significant other," to take on this powerful disease alone. Help is all around us, twenty-four hours every day, 365 days every year. Here are a few resources and how to find them:

Alcoholics Anonymous

How to Contact: Look in the yellow pages, usually under "Alcohol" or "Alcoholism."

Check the classified ads in local newspapers. The number for AA is frequently listed under "Personals," or under a similar designation.

Local newspapers may also carry the times and addresses of AA meetings, either in the classifieds or in a calendar section.

Comments: NEVER hesitate to call AA at any time, from any place, if you need help or if you're with someone who needs help. Whether you're a stranger in town, or have been fighting alcoholism for years and everybody in the local AA knows it, somebody will help you.

Al-Anon and Other Support Groups

How to Contact: Usually the same sources as for AA.

Comments: Fortunately for thousands of co-dependents, enablers, and an array of people who have various types of significant relationships with alcoholics, a number of support groups have been gaining strength, popularity, and effectiveness. Al-Anon, of course, is probably the best known of these groups, but special support organizations are available in many places for both young and adult children of alcoholics, and for victims of multiple addictions.

Treatment Centers and Detox Units

How to Contact: Most private, and many publicly funded treatment programs and detox units are listed in the yellow pages under "Alcohol," "Alcoholism," or "Alcoholism Services."

Publicly funded centers and units are often located in mental health centers and/or community health centers. If these centers don't have programs of their own they should be able to refer the caller to an appropriate resource.

Local hospitals frequently support an alcoholism unit as part of their services. Again, if the hospital doesn't have help available immediately, a referral should be provided.

Comments: Treatment centers and detox units offer a wide variety of programs for alcoholics. Some programs, obviously, are better than others, and there is a huge variation in expense. However, one should not worry about these factors when help is needed immediately. The alcoholic, or problem drinker, should be taken to the nearest facility as quickly as possible. The appropriateness of the particular program for each individual can be determined later, and a referral to another program can be made if needed.

Private Counselors

How to Contact: In the yellow pages, private counselors will usually be listed under "psychologists," "counselors," or "therapists." Rarely, however, will it be noted that the counselor treats alcoholism or chemical dependency.

Counselors may be located through the psychology and counseling departments of colleges and universities. The caller may ask for a professor who maintains a private practice and who treats chemical dependency.

Medical doctors, nurses, and other medical professionals, along with members of the clergy, are frequently acquainted with psychologists and counselors who accept referrals.

Comments: Many recovering alcoholics do not regard one-on-one counseling favorably primarily because such a setting is tailor-made for the alcoholic's conscious or subconscious manipulative skills. Traditionally, the AA approach has been more effective than individual counseling for most recovering alcoholics.

However, there are alcoholics who need more extensive help than AA may provide, once the recovery process has started. There are counselors available who are highly skilled and knowledgeable about the nature of the disease. My experience has been that the most effective private counselors combine their program of therapy with other types of group and AA support.

Clergy

How to Contact: An individual's minister, priest or rabbi may be the easiest person to contact—just go to church or pick up the telephone and call.

Comments: Despite frequent complaints (and mine are sometimes chief among them) that too many members of the clergy treat alcoholism as a moral issue, I think it's fair to say that the vast majority of the clergy have considerable insight into chemical dependency as a disease that affects entire families and entire communities. More and more are receiving specific training so they may provide counseling, and others are learning sufficient diagnostic skills to make appropriate referrals.

These are merely a few of the groups and individuals who are qualified and eager to help the victim of alcoholism. There is truly no excuse not to call for help when it is desperately needed and so readily available.

About the Author

Jerry Fite, syndicated columnist, author, and educator, served for several years in the Peace Corps as a volunteer teacher in Tunisia; as executive assistant to Peace Corps Director Sargent Shriver in Washington, D.C.; and as director of the Peace Corps program in Micronesia.

Returning to his native Southwest Missouri in 1976, he worked as a high school principal and earned his masters degree in education. He spent one year as a chemical dependency counselor at the Freeman Hospital CareUnit in Joplin, Missouri.

After serving for two years as faculty member of Pittsburg State University, Jerry is now devoting full time to his syndicated newspaper column of political humor and satire and to completing his Ph.D.

Jerry and his wife, Emmy, live in Pittsburg, Kansas, with their two children, David, seventeen, and six-year-old Melissa.